Amos, Hosea, Micah—
An Archaeological Commentary

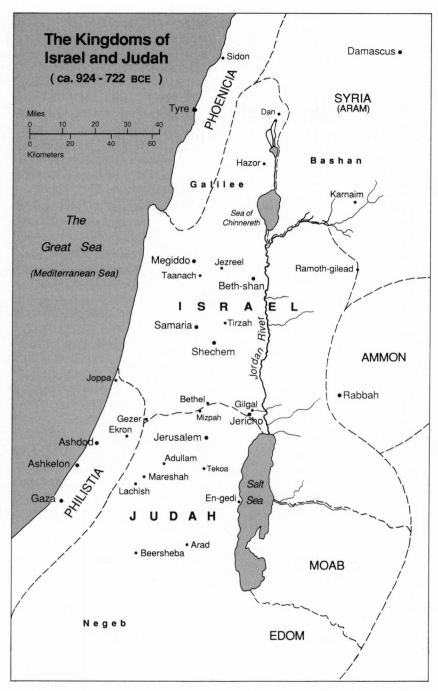

The Kingdoms of Israel and Judah

(ca. 924 - 722 BCE)

Miles

0   10   20   30   40

0   20   40   60

Kilometers

• Sidon

Damascus •

PHOENICIA

SYRIA
(ARAM)

Tyre •

Dan •

Bashan

Hazor •

Karnaim •

Galilee

*Sea of
Chinnereth*

The

Great Sea

(Mediterranean Sea)

Megiddo •

Jezreel •

Ramoth-gilead •

Taanach •

Beth-shan •

I S R A E L

Jordan River

Samaria •   •Tirzah

Shechem •

AMMON

Joppa •

Bethel •   Gilgal •

•Rabbah

Gezer •   Mizpah •

Ekron •   Jericho •

Ashdod •

Jerusalem •

Ashkelon •

Adullam •

•Tekoa

PHILISTIA

• Mareshah

Salt

Gaza •

Lachish

En-gedi •

Sea

J U D A H

• Arad

• Beersheba

MOAB

N e g e b

EDOM

Drawing by Douglas Gilbert

Amos, Hosea, Micah—
An Archaeological Commentary

Philip J. King

The Westminster Press
Philadelphia

Scripture quotations are from the Revised Standard Version of the Bible, copyrighted 1946, 1952, © 1971, 1973 by the Division of Christian Education of the National Council of the Churches of Christ in the U.S.A., and are used by permission.

Book design by Christine Schueler

Published by The Westminster Press®
Philadelphia, Pennsylvania

First edition

PRINTED IN THE UNITED STATES OF AMERICA
9 8 7 6 5 4 3 2 1

Library of Congress Cataloging-in-Publication Data

King, Philip J.
  Amos, Hosea, Micah : an archaeological commentary / Philip J.
King. — 1st ed.
      p.   cm.
  Bibliography: p.
  Includes index.
  ISBN 0-664-21876-8.   ISBN 0-664-24077-1 (pbk.)

  1. Bible. O.T. Amos—Criticism, interpretation, etc. 2. Bible.
O.T. Hosea—Criticism, interpretation, etc. 3. Bible. O.T.
Micah—Criticism, interpretation, etc. 4. Bible. O.T. Amos—
Antiquities. 5. Bible. O.T. Hosea—Antiquities. 6. Bible. O.T.
Micah—Antiquities. I. Title.
BS1560.K56 1988
224′.906—dc19   87-29539
                                                                            CIP

Contents

List of Illustrations

CHRONOLOGICAL CHART

Palestine		Mesopotamia
UNITED KINGDOM		**ASSYRIA**
David 1000–961		
Solomon 961–922		
DIVIDED KINGDOM		
JUDAH	*ISRAEL*	
Rehoboam 922–915	Jeroboam I 922–901	
		Ashurnasirpal II 884–860
	OMRIDE DYNASTY	
	Omri 876–869	
Jehoshaphat 873–849	Ahab 869–850	Shalmaneser III 859–825
Jehoram 849–842	Ahaziah 850–849	
Ahaziah 842	Jehoram 849–842	
	JEHU DYNASTY	
Athaliah 842–837	Jehu 842–815	
Joash 837–800	Jehoahaz 815–801	
Amaziah 800–783	Joash 801–786	
Uzziah 783–742	Jeroboam II 786–746	
	Zechariah 746–745	
Jotham (regent)	Shallum 745	Tiglath-pileser III 745–727
750–742		
Jotham (king) 742–735	Menahem 745–738	
	Pekahiah 738–737	
Ahaz 735–715	Pekah 737–732	
	Hoshea 732–724	
		Shalmaneser V 727–722
		Sargon II 722–705
Hezekiah 715–687		Sennacherib 704–681
Manasseh 687–642		Esarhaddon 680–669
Amon 642–640		
Josiah 640–609		Ashurbanipal 668–627
		BABYLONIA
		Nabopolassar 626–605
Jehoiakim 609–598		
Jehoiachin 598–597		Nebuchadnezzar 605–562
Zedekiah 597–587		

ARCHAEOLOGICAL PERIODS OF SYRIA-PALESTINE

Scholars are not unanimous with respect to the chronology of the ancient Near East. In the light of new archaeological evidence, chronology is constantly being refined and revised. Consequently, the dates that follow, as well as many of the dates in the text, are only approximate. For the same reason, there are occasional differences between the dates in the text and those appearing here.

Paleolithic	1,600,000–18,000 B.C.E.
Epipaleolithic	18,000–8000
Neolithic	8000–4200
Chalcolithic	4200–3300
Early Bronze/Canaanite	3300–2000
EB I (3300–3000)	
EB II (3000–2800)	
EB III (2800–2400)	
EB IV (2400–2000)	
Middle Bronze/Canaanite	2000–1550
MB I (2000–1800)	
MB II (1800–1650)	
MB III (1650–1550)	
Late Bronze/Canaanite	1550–1200
LB I (1550–1400)	
LB II (1400–1200)	
Iron/Israelite	1200–586
Iron I (1200–1000)	
Iron II (1000–586)	
Persian	538–332
Hellenistic	332–63
Roman	63 B.C.E.–324 C.E.
Byzantine	324–640

Preface

In *The Old Testament and the Archaeologist,* H. Darrell Lance, lamenting the lack of archaeological commentary on the biblical text, observes, "Most commentators do not even make use of archaeology where it can contribute best, namely in illustrating the material culture of a given period, either in general or in terms of a specific reference in the [biblical] text."[1]

When I completed my term as president of the American Schools of Oriental Research and was seeking a new challenge, Michael Coogan suggested that I respond to the need that Lance expresses by writing a commentary on the eighth-century prophets Amos, Hosea, and Micah (Isaiah would be a book by itself) from an archaeological perspective. Having earlier done a more traditional commentary on Amos and Micah,[2] I found the subject matter appealing. My formal academic training in Hebrew Bible (Old Testament) and my extensive field experience in archaeology appeared to be the proper combination for undertaking such a project.

Thanks to the knowledge explosion, archaeology and Bible are such vast academic disciplines today that a scholar works with some apprehension in either one or the other; for a scholar to attempt to work in both is downright brash. Were it not for the assurance and assistance coming from several archaeologists and biblical scholars, all personal friends, I would not have undertaken this commentary. It is a pleasure to acknowledge at least some of these scholars by name: Michael Coogan, Lawrence Stager, and Carl Graesser, who read the manuscript at various stages and made valuable observations; Trude Dothan and Ephraim Stern, who suggested most of the graphics that appear in this book. I wish also to thank Arnold and Amalie Flegenheimer, who generously funded the preparation of the photographs and illustrations for publication, and Cynthia Thompson of The Westminster Press for her professional assistance at every stage in the preparation of this book. I have used the Revised Standard Version for scripture quotations, and all references follow its verse numbering. For convenience, however, poetry quotations are set as prose. Hebrew words are usually cited in a simple form, not necessarily in the form appearing in the biblical text. "Tel," the Hebrew equivalent of the Arabic "Tell," designates archaeological sites in modern Israel.

It is my pleasant duty to acknowledge the generous grant from the National Endowment for the Humanities that made it possible for me to spend an extended period at the Albright Institute of Archaeological Research in Jerusalem, where most of the research for this archaeological commentary was conducted. While I was resident in Jerusalem, Israeli archaeologists, too numerous to mention, were constantly available for consultation; they also generously provided photographs, as the List of Illustrations attests.

A work of synthesis such as the present book must depend upon the results of others' research, as the accompanying notes and selected bibliography only mildly suggest. Those familiar with archaeology and biblical studies will immediately recognize the sources of this book. Those with less specialized interest in these subjects will not wish to be encumbered by scholarly detail. If each group finds some benefit in these pages, the writing of them will have been worthwhile.

Introduction

The past two decades have seen the appearance of a spate of traditional commentaries devoted for the most part to literary, rhetorical, theological, and philological considerations surrounding the biblical text. During this same period, archaeological work in the forms of excavations and surveys has been proceeding in the biblical lands at an unprecedented rate. Nonetheless the archaeological factor has been slighted in the biblical commentaries; it is surely the great untapped resource. The fact that archaeological reports often appear in journals not readily available to biblical scholars may partly explain this neglect.

Biblical archaeology is a biblical, not an archaeological, discipline. Therefore it is the responsibility of biblical scholars, not of archaeologists, to ferret out pertinent information and apply it to the Bible. To cite William F. Albright's broad definition, biblical archaeology "is the systematic analysis or synthesis of any phase of biblical scholarship which can be clarified by archaeological discovery."[1]

Today's need is for works of synthesis that bring the archaeological data to bear on the biblical text. The integration of the two can add much to the understanding of the Bible. Archaeology continues to be useful for placing the Bible in the historical and geographical context of the ancient Near East. Today, however, a shift is taking place from exclusively historical interests to anthropological issues dealing with the life and culture of ancient peoples. With models taken from the social sciences, the archaeological record can be utilized now to reconstruct the social organization of biblical society.[2]

Sometimes the Bible is ambiguous, tendentious, or unintelligible; at such times archaeology may be able to clarify, supplement, or correct the biblical text. Of course, archaeology too has its limitations; the artifacts it unearths are often mute, ambiguous, or anonymous, making them subject to a variety of interpretations.

This book focuses on artifacts and other material remains recovered through excavation and survey, with the hope that they may illuminate the eighth-century prophets Amos, Hosea, and Micah; for this reason it may be called an archaeological commentary. The text is supplemented with photographs and other illustrations to give greater clarity and to demonstrate that the Bible is concerned with people who really lived.

After the concepts of archaeology and prophetism are considered, some of the main forms, constantly alluded to by the prophets, in which the social life of biblical people found expression are discussed: urbanization, architecture, warfare, industry, and religion.

The present work may answer only a few questions about the eighth-century prophets, but it may raise some new ones as well.

1

Archaeology
and the Eighth-Century Prophets

The principal purpose of this book is to promote a dialogue between archaeology and the biblical text, specifically the eighth-century prophets, for a better understanding of the Bible. This chapter deals with preliminary ideas about archaeology and the prophets. The first part includes the definition of archaeology and its relationship to biblical archaeology, followed by a brief history of the discipline. The second part treats the nature of prophetism, followed by a brief biography of the eighth-century prophets Amos, Hosea, and Micah, the major themes of each, and an outline of their books. Midway between the discussion of archaeology and the prophets is a brief statement about focus, method, and scope, which moves from archaeology to the text of the eighth-century prophets.

Although the Bible is well known, it is not well understood, because it is removed in both time and place from the modern Western reader. Whatever helps to clarify the Bible, therefore, is always welcome. Linguistic, rhetorical, and literary studies are making a meaningful contribution to the understanding of the Bible. Archaeology too has much to offer, but to date it has been somewhat slighted.

Archaeology, defined as the scientific study of the material remains of past human life and activities, is a comprehensive discipline, encompassing both written (epigraphic) and unwritten (nonepigraphic) discoveries. Although inscriptions and texts of all kinds have been recovered through archaeological excavations, archaeology is usually limited to the analysis of material evidence, while the decipherment of texts is left to other disciplines.

The Bible and archaeology are so closely related that "biblical archaeology" has become a household term. It is a biblical discipline whose purpose is to gain insight into the Bible. Simply defined, biblical archaeology is the process of correlating archaeological evidence with the biblical record in order to illuminate the biblical text. The combination of material evidence derived through archaeology and of textual data provided by literary scholarship can add significantly to the understanding of the Bible. Archaeological realia—that is, the residues of human activity and creativity, also known as material culture—bring an important new dimension to the study of the biblical text.

The archaelogical contribution to biblical studies can no longer be neglected, especially in view of the extraordinary amount of archaeological fieldwork in progress today in the Middle East, the environment in which the Bible took shape. Syro-Palestinian archaeology, as it is called, which includes biblical archaeology, has developed phenomenally in both conception and method during its relatively short history, spanning less than a century.

The Beginnings of Biblical Archaeology

Tracing its roots to the mid-nineteenth century, Syro-Palestinian archaeology received its great impetus from the American biblical scholar Edward Robinson, who in the course of two historic trips to the Middle East (1838 and 1852) was able to identify over one hundred biblical sites. The goal of his journeys was the study of the physical and historical geography of the Holy Land (Palestine). To emphasize the strong biblical component of his undertakings, Robinson published the results in a multivolume work entitled *Biblical Researches in Palestine.*

The establishment in 1865 of the Palestine Exploration Fund, a British society for the systematic and scientific exploration of Palestine, was a direct consequence of Robinson's travels. In addition to the scientific mapping of Jerusalem, the Palestine Exploration Fund was responsible for geographical surveys on both sides of the Jordan River.

The first systematic excavation in Palestine was conducted in 1890 by the British Egyptologist W. M. Flinders Petrie. Unlike Robinson, he understood that the artificial mounds, or tells (tels, in Hebrew), that dot the Syro-Palestinian landscape contain the remains of earlier human occupation. At Tell el-Hesi, Petrie laid the foundations of stratigraphy and ceramic typology, the twin principles of archaeological method for Palestine. Briefly, the stratigraphic method of digging is concerned with untangling a tell's superimposed layers, or strata (similar to a layer cake), which represent successive occupational levels of a tell. The oldest occupation is found at the bottom of the tell and the latest or most recent at the top. Ceramic typology denotes the classification of the large quantities of broken pottery, excellent indicators of ancient chronology, which are found within the strata of a tell. The fact that pottery styles differ in the successive strata of a mound indicates an evolution of pottery types. These stylistic changes in the pottery can be classified and dated; in turn, the strata or occupational levels can be dated by the pottery found in them.

The American Schools of Oriental Research, a professional organization established in 1900 to promote biblical, linguistic, archaeological, and historical studies in the Middle East, has encouraged and supported most of the American scholars working in these disciplines throughout this century.

One of the significant digs before World War I took place at Samaria from 1908 to 1910. A prominent city in the eighth century B.C.E., Samaria was the capital of the Northern Kingdom of Israel. In the course of this first American dig in Palestine, George Reisner, director at Samaria, made a permanent contribution to excavation technique in Palestine by his concern for precision in digging and recording. Benefiting from several improvements by later archaeologists, especially Kathleen Kenyon of England, the Reisner method is still in use today.

Archaeology Between World Wars I and II

Among the great excavations of this period were Samaria, Megiddo, Lachish, Tell Beit Mirsim, Tell en-Nasbeh, and Beth-shemesh. These sites laid the foundation for all later archaeological investigations.

Between World Wars I and II, James Breasted of the University of Chicago was responsible for a monumental dig at Megiddo, a well-planned and prosperous city in the Northern Kingdom of Israel during the eighth century B.C.E. In all, the excavators distinguished twenty occupational periods at Megiddo, dating from about 3300 to 300 B.C.E.

William F. Albright, one of the outstanding leaders of the American Schools of Oriental Research, contributed more than any of his peers and his successors to the advancement of biblical archaeology. He defined and refined pottery chronology through excavation and survey; he identified several tells as biblical sites; he deciphered ancient texts relating to the Bible and related many of the textual episodes to archaeological contexts. He was responsible for interplay and dialogue between texts and archaeology for narrative history. In short, Albright was involved in every aspect of biblical and archaeological studies until his death in 1971. Seldom has one person so influenced a scholarly discipline.

Archaeology After World War II

This period is marked especially by the improvement in excavation technique. The history of Syro-Palestinian archaeology following World War II can be summarized in the achievements of three international leaders: Kathleen Kenyon, Yigael Yadin, and G. Ernest Wright. Concentrating on the layer-by-layer exposure of a mound, Kenyon emphasized stratigraphy, which she combined with careful recording of the remains. Her work at Jericho, a model of field method, clarified several nagging problems of history and chronology; she established that the Jericho village was destroyed about 1400 B.C.E.

Yadin, emphasizing the horizontal or broad exposure of a tell, conducted among other projects the excavation at Hazor; this was the first major project by Israeli archaeologists after the establishment of the State of Israel. The largest city in Palestine during biblical times, Hazor was destroyed by the Assyrians in the eighth century B.C.E. Hazor, Samaria, and Megiddo were the most important sites in the Northern Kingdom of Israel during Iron Age II (1000–586 B.C.E.).

During his excavations at Shechem, the first capital of the Northern Kingdom of Israel, Wright trained his American students, many of whom were to become prominent archaeologists. While profiting from the methods of both Kenyon and Yadin, Wright made his own contribution to Palestinian archaeology, especially in pottery chronology, which he made more precise.

The Arab-Israeli war of 1967 occasioned major changes in archaeology, as it did also in geographical borders and history. It appeared to increase the number of excavations on both sides of the Jordan River, that is, in Israel and Jordan, as well as in several of the neighboring Arab countries. So many digs have been conducted during the past twenty years that it would be tedious to list them. Some of the most significant field projects, three especially, centered on Jerusalem, one of the most excavated cities in the world: Benjamin Mazar's dig at the Temple Mount, Nahman Avigad's in the Jewish Quarter, and Yigal Shiloh's in the City of David. These projects have revealed more about Jerusalem than all previous digs combined.

The centerpiece of biblical archaeology, today as in antiquity, is Jerusalem. Established by King David as the capital of the United Kingdom (1000–922 B.C.E.), Jerusalem was prominent in that era as well as during the period of the Divided Kingdom (922–586 B.C.E.). As archaeology and the prophets attest, in the eighth century B.C.E. the city was enlarged and its defenses strengthened.

Biblical Archaeology Today

Today archaeology is utilizing more sophisticated methods of research borrowed from both the natural and the social sciences, as evidenced by the composition of the staff of most excavations in Israel and Jordan. Such specialists as paleobotanists, zooarchaeologists, geologists, hydrologists, and anthropologists work in collaboration with the archaeologists. Also, modern scientific technologies such as remote sensing, magnetometry, and neutron activation analysis, to name a few, provide more precise analysis of data. The methods and data of the social sciences are also playing an important role today in analyzing the archaeological evidence and in interpreting the biblical texts. These newer techniques and methods make it possible for Syro-Palestinian archaeology to go beyond its earlier concern with political history (wars, kings, etc.) and now to gain an understanding of social history as well.

The ideal of biblical archaeology is to reconstruct every aspect of the life and thought of ancient Israel, including social structure, economic development, and trade patterns. Reconstructing the social setting of biblical people leads to a clearer understanding of their writings. With respect to the eighth century B.C.E., this more comprehensive approach to archaeology is providing information about the development of agriculture, trade, and industry, which indirectly created the pyramidal social structure in Israel against which the prophets inveighed so vehemently.

Archaeology and the Bible

If archaeology is to contribute meaningfully to biblical studies, an ongoing dialogue between the disciplines is indispensable. Correlating archaeological data with the biblical record is a deceptively simple description of biblical archaeology; the artifacts are often mute, and the biblical text is sometimes ambiguous, tendentious, or even unintelligible to the modern interpreter, many centuries removed from the original sociocultural environment that (along with genius) produced them. Nonetheless archaeological evidence can contribute to the understanding of the biblical text by confirming, correcting, or supplementing it. At the same time, the text must be subjected to form-critical, tradition-historical, and other kinds of analysis.

In sum, archaeology contributes to biblical studies by establishing the general setting of the biblical events in the ancient Near East and by reconstructing the life and culture of biblical times, specifically in the social, economic, and religious realms.

The Present Work

This present work utilizes the material culture of Iron Age II (1000–586 B.C.E.), recovered through archaeology, to illustrate the texts of the eighth-century prophets Amos, Hosea, and Micah. The large amount of pertinent evidence now available is most useful in reconstructing the life and culture of ancient Israel at the time of the prophets. The sources of information that archaeology makes available are varied: house plans, cultic objects, decorative pottery, weapons of war, and musical instruments, to name a few. When the prophetic texts refer to such realia as these, their physical appearance often is not described, but archaeology can usually fill in the gaps. For the most part, the present work deals with material evidence drawn from Iron Age II, except when artifacts from other periods may be especially useful. With few exceptions, the material remains considered in this work do not include written documents but are limited to unwritten or artifactual evidence. In addition to illustrating the historical aspects of the eighth century B.C.E., to the extent possible, the artifacts are analyzed for the insights they offer into the social and economic life of the Israelites of that era. The main purpose of this work, then, is to analyze data different from literary evidence, data deriving from archaeology, for a better understanding of the Bible.

The Biblical Prophets

Prophetism did not originate in Israel; older civilizations also had their prophets. Nor were the eighth-century prophets Amos, Hosea, and Micah the first to appear in Israel; they too had their forerunners. Amos, Hosea, and Micah are often called minor prophets because their oracles are not preserved in great quantity when compared with the so-called major prophets Isaiah, Jeremiah, and Ezekiel. In fact, with respect to influence on society, no prophet was minor. It is important to understand that the oracles of the prophets were transmitted orally, with the result that the prophetic books are anthologies or collections rather than coherent literary works.

The Hebrew word *nabi'*, translated "prophet," means "one who announces." The Greek word *prophētēs* (from which "prophet" is derived) designates "one who speaks for another." The prophets, then, were not forecasters but were God's mouthpieces; their primary function was to proclaim, not to predict. The prophets were not innovators; they were reformers who constantly reminded the Israelites of their covenant obligations. Although they uttered threats, the prophets also offered hope, provided the people would repent. The principal mission of the prophets was religious, but it was intimately related to politics, because the two can never be separated.

The Book of Amos

Outline
Oracles against the nations (Amos 1–2)
Indictment of the Northern Kingdom of Israel (Amos 3–6)
Impending doom of Israel (Amos 7–9)

Biographical data about the prophet Amos are sketchy. The biblical text mentions only that he was a herdsman (Amos 1:1) and a dresser of sycamore trees (Amos 7:14). Although he came from the village of Tekoa about ten miles south of Jerusalem, he preached in the Northern Kingdom of Israel, where he was associated with the capital city of Samaria and the royal sanctuary at Bethel, from which he was expelled by the priest Amaziah (Amos 7:10–17). Acknowledging the universal sovereignty of Israel's God, Amos was vitally aware of the political events in the neighboring nations as well as in Israel. Active at a time of peace during the prosperous reigns of King Uzziah of Judah (783–742 B.C.E.) and King Jeroboam II of Israel (786–746 B.C.E.), Amos appears to have exercised his prophetic ministry for only a short period of time.

The Book of Amos has several allusions to an earthquake, which may indicate precisely when he functioned as a prophet. The opening verse has a specific reference: "The words of Amos, who was among the shepherds of Tekoa, which he saw concerning Israel in the days of Uzziah king of Judah and in the days of Jeroboam the son of Joash, king of Israel, two years before the earthquake" (Amos 1:1). This earthquake is also mentioned in Zech. 14:5. The earthquake would seem to pinpoint Amos' ministry, and some archaeologists think they have found evidence of it, although it cannot be dated precisely.

On the basis of pottery, Yadin dated Stratum VI at Hazor to the eighth century B.C.E. He also concluded that this stratum was destroyed by an earthquake: "Many walls in this stratum were found bent or crooked: in several places we found debris of walls lying course on course, just as is found in earthquakes when the entire wall collapses at once."[1] Yohanan Aharoni, excavator of Beer-sheba, conjectured that the destruction of Stratum III at this site may have been caused by the same earthquake.

Amos, the first prophet whose oracles and visions have been preserved in written form, appears to have been a rugged outdoorsman who preached divine judgment with harsh severity. Influenced by the tradition of the Mosaic covenant, which is based not on privilege but on responsibility, Amos was deeply disturbed by the rampant social

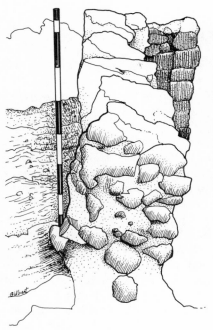

Evidence of an earthquake at Hazor. Tilted walls in Stratum VI (first half of the eighth century B.C.E.) point to the destruction of Hazor by earthquake. Like Amos (1:1), Zechariah mentions an earthquake "in the days of Uzziah king of Judah" (Zech. 14:5). This earthquake apparently made a lasting impression. *(Courtesy of the Expedition to Hazor, Yigael Yadin, Director; drawing by Douglas Gilbert)*

injustice perpetrated by his contemporaries, especially the venal upper class.

Israel, at peace with Judah, was at the zenith of its power; economic prosperity was evident everywhere: in commerce, trade, and building activities. Contrary to the Mosaic covenant, wealth had created a social imbalance, which resulted in two separate classes, the rich and the poor. Those at the top of the pyramid exploited the weak and oppressed the poor by alienation of land, forced labor, and heavy taxes. Amos protested bitterly against the perversion of justice among the Israelites. He went so far as to say that as punishment the "day of the Lord" would not be a day of vindication (as traditionally thought) but of inevitable doom: "Woe to you who desire the day of the LORD! Why would you have the day of the LORD? It is darkness, and not light" (Amos 5:18). Among the concrete examples of oppression inflicted on the poor, the following two are typical. One concerns weights and measures, the other pledged garments.

Weights and Measures

Falsifying weights and measures was a flagrant abuse of justice in the eighth century B.C.E., and Amos, Hosea, and Micah all roundly condemned it.

In indicting the fraudulent merchants who were manipulating the scales and falsifying the weights, Amos quotes their importunate questions: "When will the new moon be over, that we may sell grain? And the sabbath, that we may offer wheat for sale, that we may make the ephah small and the shekel great, and deal deceitfully with false balances?" (Amos 8:5).

Hosea refers to deceitful Israel, unfaithful to covenant requirements, as "a trader, in whose hands are false balances, he loves to oppress" (Hos. 12:7). Micah quotes the Lord's words to the people of Jerusalem and the Southern Kingdom: "Shall I acquit the man with wicked scales and with a bag of deceitful weights?" (Micah 6:11). Apparently the fraudulent practices of the Northern Kingdom had corrupted Judah as well.

Israelite law prescribes honest weights and measures: "You shall not have in your bag two kinds of weights, a large and a small. You shall not have in your house two kinds of measures, a large and a small. A full and just weight you shall have, a full and just measure you shall have" (Deut. 25:13–15).

Textual ambiguities and limited archaeological discoveries leave unanswered some questions about biblical metrology (the science of weights and measures), which was not an exact science anyway; more information is available about weights than measures. The Hebrew system of weights and measures appears to have been developed from the Babylonian system. The balance, a basic instrument for determining weights, consisted of a beam hung from a cord held in the hand or fitted to an upright support; from each end of the beam a pan was suspended by cords. The balance weights were usually made of hard stone.

The standard unit of weight was the shekel, calculated at slightly over eleven grams. "Shekel" comes from the Hebrew root *shql*, meaning "to weigh." Shekels could be either uninscribed or inscribed, the latter dating for the most part from the eighth and seventh centuries B.C.E., owing perhaps to the reforms of Hezekiah and Josiah, kings of Judah. A loop resembling a figure 8 symbolized the shekel. This looped symbol may represent the *seror* or "tied bundle" used for carrying silver, which was the medium of exchange.

The ephah, an Egyptian word probably meaning "basket," was the most common unit of dry measure. Used in measuring the grain being sold, the ephah could refer to the quantity of grain or to the container in which the grain was measured. The ephah is computed as three fifths of a U.S. bushel. The homer, a standard unit of dry measure in the Bible, equals ten ephah. Literally an ass, the homer is equivalent to the load that this beast of burden could carry.

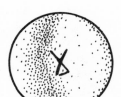
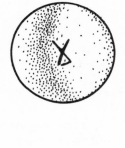
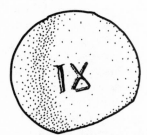

Weights from Tel Miqne (Ekron). These weights, averaging about one inch in diameter, date to the late seventh century B.C.E. In the lower left is a five-shekel weight; in the center a two-shekel weight; in the upper right a beka (half-shekel weight). The looped symbol of the shekel may represent the tied sack in which the silver was carried. *(Courtesy of the Joint Excavation Project, Trude Dothan and Seymour Gitin, Directors; drawing by Douglas Gilbert)*

Pledged Garments

Among the accusations against Israel, the Lord charges: "They lay themselves down beside every altar upon garments taken in pledge" (Amos 2:8). An Israelite could secure a debt by handing over his garment. At the same time, the debtor had the right to expect the return of the garment. In the case of the poor, this was critical, because the pledged garment also served as a covering against the cold of the night. The covenant code explicitly states: "If ever you take your neighbor's garment in pledge, you shall restore it to him before the sun goes down; for that is his only covering, it is his mantle for his body; in what else shall he sleep?" (Ex. 22:26–27). The most frequently used Hebrew word for a garment is *beged* (Amos 2:8); another common word with a general meaning is *simlah* (Ex. 22:27). These two words among others designate the cloak worn over the tunic; it was the cloak that served as a covering at night.

Inside the guardroom of a small fortress at Meṣad Ḥashavyahu, situated in modern Israel on the coast close to Yavneh-yam, a four-teen-line Hebrew ostracon (an inscribed potsherd) was discovered in 1960. Dating from about 625 B.C.E., in the reign of King Josiah when the fortress was under the control of Judah, this letter was from a reaper who complained that his garment *(beged)* had been impounded. Maintaining innocence, he asked the military governor to intervene for the return of the garment. Why it was seized is uncertain; perhaps the aggrieved person had not completed his quota of the harvest. As a

Hebrew letter from Meṣad Hashavyahu. This ostracon dating to the
second half of the seventh century B.C.E. contains fourteen lines of biblical
Hebrew written in ink. Found inside a guardroom, it is an official
complaint by a reaper that his garment had been confiscated unjustly.
*(Courtesy of the Israel Department of Antiquities; photo by David Harris, Israel
Museum, Jerusalem)*

nonbiblical document dealing with everyday life in Judah before the
exile (586 B.C.E.), this inscription is of special value.

The Book of Hosea

Outline

Hosea's marriage to Gomer (Hosea 1–3)
Judgment and salvation oracles (Hosea 4–14)

Biographical information about Hosea, the younger contemporary
of Amos, is quite meager. He married Gomer, who was either a temple
prostitute or an unfaithful spouse. Their three children were given
symbolic names: a son Jezreel ("God sows"), a daughter Not-Pitied
(*Lo-ruhamah*), and another son, Not-My-People (*Lo-'ammi*). These

names foreshadowed the destruction of the Northern Kingdom of
Israel for violation of the divine covenant. Hosea's prophetic career
may have extended over three decades, from the last years of Jeroboam II (786–746 B.C.E.) to the fall of Samaria in 721 B.C.E. He seems
to have had firsthand information of the Syro-Israelite war in 735–734
B.C.E.

Hosea was master of the metaphor, often using flora and fauna to
make his theological points. He speaks of the divine-human relationship in familial terms of father-son and husband-wife. For Hosea,
marital imagery symbolized the covenant relationship between God
and Israel. Reading between the lines, one has the impression that
Hosea was sensitive and emotional, perhaps even brokenhearted over
his domestic tragedy.

Hosea opposed, if not to the same degree as Amos, the socioeco-
nomic abuses of his day. He was especially angered by the prophets,
priests, and kings for misleading the people. Interested exclusively in
his own people, Hosea did not address oracles to foreign nations. His
principal concern was with Israel's religious apostasy, which was especially shocking owing to God's great love for Israel. No prophet was
more profoundly aware of the depth of divine love and its indestructi-
bility, as Hosea 11 bears eloquent witness. If John is the evangelist of
love in the New Testament, Hosea is the prophet of love in the Old.
Hosea became an outspoken critic of Israel's fertility cult because it
was a betrayal of God's great love for Israel.

Among the literary prophets, Hosea was the only native of the
Northern Kingdom of Israel. He was deeply immersed in the Mosaic
tradition, with its themes of deliverance from Egypt and of God's
concern for the nation in the wilderness. Hosea preached hope of
renewal, but only after destruction of the nation and repentance of the
people. To express hope in the future, he utilized the "second exodus–
conquest" motif; what God had done in the first exodus, God would
do again. He quoted the Lord: "Therefore, behold, I will allure her
[Israel], and bring her into the wilderness, and speak tenderly to her.
And there I will give her her vineyards, and make the Valley of Achor
a door of hope" (Hos. 2:14–15).

The Valley of Achor

The Buqeah ("little valley") lies in a desolate sector of the Judean
hills, southwest of Jericho. In biblical times this valley was known as
Achor (literally, "valley of trouble"). Here, during the conquest of
Canaan, Achan and his family were stoned to death, on orders from
Joshua, for transgressing the divine command to take no booty from

Jericho. According to Hosea's prophecy, this treacherous valley would be transformed into a "door of hope" (Heb.: *petah tiqvah*). The oldest Jewish agricultural settlement in Palestine, founded in 1878 and situated seven miles from modern Tel Aviv, is named Petah Tiqvah, after the prophecy of Hosea. Originally the settlers wanted to build their colony in the Valley of Achor, but it was not possible. Today Petah Tiqvah is a center of citrus culture.

In 1955 Frank Cross and Jozef Milik made a limited survey of the Buqeah, concentrating on three fortresses that were thought to date to the ninth-eighth century B.C.E. In 1972 Lawrence Stager made a more intensive study of the Buqeah, determining that the forts and their floodwater farms dated actually to the seventh century B.C.E. and were paramilitary outposts for protecting the desert farmer-soldiers as well as travelers on their way between Moab (in Transjordan) and Jerusalem. But more important, these outposts in the wilderness secured the route by which such essential natural resources from the Dead Sea as salt, sulfur, and bitumen were transported to Jerusalem. Irrigation agriculture was possible in this wilderness by the use of sluice gates and terrace dams to control the floodwaters of the valley. Perhaps Hosea's metaphor about the transformation of the Valley of Achor into a "door of hope" was not so farfetched after all.

The Book of Micah

Outline

Judgment against the nations and leaders (Micah 1–3)
Restoration of Zion (Micah 4–5)
Lawsuit against Israel, followed by an expression of hope
  (Micah 6–7)

Micah was a native of the obscure border village of Moresheth-gath in Judah, not far from the Philistine city of Gath and about twenty miles southwest of Jerusalem. A younger contemporary of Isaiah, he was a rural prophet who lived during the last quarter of the eighth century B.C.E. It was a period of political crisis and a time of intense economic pressure for the people of Judah. The incursions of the Assyrians and finally the defeat of Judah at their hands in 701 B.C.E. meant that huge sums had to be invested in arms and fortifications, and tribute had to be rendered to Assyria. Also, following the demise of the Northern Kingdom two decades earlier (721 B.C.E.), the Southern Kingdom was burdened by a great influx of Israelites from Samaria.

Though little is known of Micah's life, his message is exceedingly clear. He identified with the poor and weak, for whom he had deep sympathy. This blunt "Amos of the Southern Kingdom" preached social justice, strongly defending the rights of small farmers, whose lands were being expropriated. Micah too was a vigorous critic of the unjust leaders—priests, prophets, judges—who exploited the people mercilessly.

Against the Political and Religious Leaders

In an announcement of judgment against the corrupt public officials in Jerusalem, Micah, quoting the words of the Lord, portrays them as butchers and cannibals:

> Hear, you heads of Jacob and rulers of the house of Israel! Is it not for you to know justice?—you who hate the good and love the evil, who tear the skin from off my people, and their flesh from off their bones; who eat the flesh of my people, and flay their skin from off them, and break their bones in pieces, and chop them up like meat in a kettle, like flesh in a caldron. (Micah 3:1–3)

The Covenant Lawsuit (Micah 6:1–8)

One of the most memorable passages of Micah is the covenant lawsuit (*rib*) in which the Lord is the plaintiff and Judah the defendant. In making the case against Judah for violating the covenant, the Lord recalls Israel's history, with the exodus at its center: "For I brought you up from the land of Egypt, and redeemed you from the house of bondage; and I sent before you Moses, Aaron, and Miriam. O my people, remember what Balak king of Moab devised, and what Balaam[2] the son of Beor answered him, and what happened from Shittim to Gilgal, that you may know the saving acts of the LORD" (Micah 6:4–5). Although a native of the Southern Kingdom, Micah favored the exodus tradition of Sinai over the court theology of the Davidic dynasty.

This lawsuit ends with a single sentence which epitomizes prophetic religion and sums up the theology of the eighth-century prophets: "He [the LORD] has showed you, O man, what is good; and what does the Lord require of you but to do justice, and to love kindness (*hesed*), and to walk humbly with your God?" (Micah 6:8).

Micah and Jerusalem

Micah, unlike Isaiah, prophesied the destruction of Jerusalem (Micah 3:9–12), a fact that was recalled a century later during the trial of Jeremiah and cited in his defense (Jer. 26:18).

2

Historical
and Geographical Setting

The purpose of this chapter is to situate the eighth-century prophets historically and geographically in preparation for understanding their messages, which were directed to their contemporaries. Inasmuch as the divided Kingdoms of Israel and Judah did not function in isolation, it is important to know something about the nations with whom they interacted, both in peace and in war. The prominent cities of the Northern and the Southern Kingdom mentioned by the eighth-century prophets are discussed in some detail. Amos directs several of his oracles against the neighboring nations; each of these nations is discussed. One of Micah's laments mentions the towns surrounding his own, Moresheth-gath; these towns are also considered.

Historical Background of the Eighth Century B.C.E.

As people of their own times and places, Amos, Hosea, and Micah cannot be separated from the history and geography of the Near East in the eighth century B.C.E. With this awareness, the editors of the three prophets record in the opening verse of each prophetic book the reigning kings, including Jeroboam II of the Northern Kingdom of Israel as well as Uzziah, Jotham, Ahaz, and Hezekiah of the Southern Kingdom of Judah. These monarchs had the most prominent roles, but other leaders from Judah and Israel, as well as leaders from neighboring Syria and Assyria, had their part to play.

Only after the death of King Solomon in 922 B.C.E. did Israel and Judah become separate political entities. Previously the name Israel designated the United Kingdom. After the schism of 922 B.C.E., the Northern Kingdom became known as Israel (also referred to as Ephraim, especially by Hosea), and the Southern Kingdom was called Judah. When the modern Jewish state was established in 1948 following the partition of Palestine, it too was called Israel.

The fortunes of Judah and Israel depended almost exclusively on their neighbors, especially Syria (Aram) and Assyria. When the neighbors were weak, Israel and Judah prospered. In the first half of the eighth century B.C.E., owing to Syria's decline of power and Assyria's turmoil at home, Judah and Israel prospered. On the other hand, when Judah and Israel were not feuding with their neighbors, they were often at war with each other.

Because of their geographic proximity Israel and Syria were natural rivals. But Assyria was the greater threat because of its imperial ambitions. In the first half of the eighth century B.C.E., Assyria was hampered by internal problems; in the second half, that situation changed. Appearing on the scene in 745 B.C.E., King Tiglath-pileser III was bent on expanding the Assyrian empire.

Owing to the fact that it was always ruled by the Davidic dynasty, Judah was a more stable nation than the Northern Kingdom of Israel; some of the outstanding kings of Israel belonged to the Omride and Jehu dynasties. The Omride dynasty came to a bloody end when Jehu conducted a purge against Israel in 842 B.C.E. He proceeded to the town of Jezreel, at the foot of Mt. Gilboa, where he killed King Jehoram of Israel, Jezebel, and the remaining members of Ahab's family (2 Kings 9–10). Then Jehu became king of Israel.

During the period of Assyrian weakness both Israel and Judah had strong kings who enjoyed long reigns: Jeroboam II of Israel (786–746 B.C.E.) and Uzziah (Azariah) of Judah (783–742 B.C.E.). The accession of their fathers, Joash of Israel and Amaziah of Judah, had coincided with the beginning of the eighth century B.C.E. Despite his reconquest of Edom, Amaziah was no match for Joash. He made the fatal error of challenging Joash, who responded by demolishing a portion of Jerusalem's wall, looting the Temple and the palace treasury, taking hostages to Samaria, and in the end reducing Judah to vassalage. As a consequence, despite the outstanding leadership of Amaziah's son and successor Uzziah, Judah continued to be overshadowed by the Northern Kingdom of Israel during the reign of Jeroboam II, Joash's son and successor.

Jeroboam II of Israel (786–746 B.C.E.)

Without question, Jeroboam II was the greatest king of the Jehu dynasty. Unhampered by Assyria, Jeroboam II was able to expand the borders of Israel; he may have regained control over Transjordan and parts of Syria, including Damascus, although the textual evidence is not clear. Alluding to Israel's military victories, Amos mentions two cities in Transjordan captured by Israel: "You who rejoice in Lo-debar,

who say, 'Have we not by our own strength taken Karnaim for our-
selves?' " (Amos 6:13). These two Transjordanian cities controlled
major routes east of the Jordan River. It may be that Amos was making
a deliberate wordplay on the names of these cities: Lo-debar suggests
"nothing," and Karnaim "horns," a metaphor for strength. The tribute received from these conquered peoples, as well as the newly acquired land, made Israel a prosperous nation, but it also occasioned
social injustice and rank exploitation at home, as Amos continuously
points out.

Amos' undisguised threats against Jeroboam II attest to the con-
tempt in which he held the king. In the vision of the plumb line, Amos
quotes the Lord as saying, "I will rise against the house of Jeroboam
with the sword" (Amos 7:9). Likewise, in his encounter with Amaziah,
the priest of Bethel, Amos is reported to have said, "Jeroboam shall
die by the sword" (Amos 7:11). Hosea shared Amos' negative senti-
ments; he quotes the Lord in the same menacing terms on the occasion
of naming the first child of Hosea and Gomer: "Call his name Jezreel;
for yet a little while, and I will punish the house of Jehu for the blood
of Jezreel, and I will put an end to the kingdom of the house of Israel"
(Hos. 1:4). Recalling this massacre at the hands of Jehu a century after
the event, Hosea prophesied that the Lord would punish the Jehu
dynasty, whose reigning king in Hosea's time was Jeroboam II.

Uzziah of Judah (783–742 B.C.E.)

Uzziah (Azariah), Jeroboam's contemporary in Judah, brought his
country to the zenith of its power through expansion and military
might, though it remained dependent upon the Northern Kingdom of
Israel. Besides having military successes over Philistia and Edom, Uzziah was an excellent administrator, who developed agriculture by
establishing military-agricultural settlements in the Negev (or Negeb;
the southern part of Judah), which in turn protected the trade routes.
When Uzziah was afflicted with leprosy, his son Jotham served as
regent for eight years (750–742 B.C.E.). Afterward, reigning in his own
name Jotham (742–735 B.C.E.) continued the undertakings of his father, including the strengthening of Jerusalem's fortifications and
other building activities elsewhere in the kingdom.

Tiglath-pileser III of Assyria (745–727 B.C.E.)

The unprecedented peace, power, and prosperity that Judah and
Israel had enjoyed were brought to an abrupt end in 745 B.C.E. by
Tiglath-pileser III of Assyria. His accession to the throne marked the

Tiglath-pileser III in triumph. This relief is from Nimrud, about 730
B.C.E. Under Tiglath-pileser III the Assyrian empire expanded into Syria
and the northern part of Israel. *(Courtesy of the Trustees of the British Museum)*

beginning of a century of Assyrian imperialism, which finally came to an end with the Babylonian defeat of the Assyrians in 609 B.C.E., but only after Assyria had subjugated almost the whole Near East. Annexation and deportation were integral parts of Assyrian expansion, accomplished by a brutal army expert in siege warfare. Conquered people were deported and their land incorporated into the Assyrian empire. All the nations west of the Euphrates River were in fear of Tiglath-pileser III, who was bent on control of the trade routes in that region. His first expedition to Palestine was in 734 B.C.E., when he directed a campaign against Philistia (the coastal plain of Palestine, including Ashdod, Ashkelon, Ekron, Gath, and Gaza) and conquered Gaza. His second military operation, in 733 B.C.E., aimed at the Northern Kingdom of Israel, resulted in the conquest of the cities of Hazor (Stratum V), which was completely destroyed, and Megiddo (Stratum IV), and the regions of Galilee and Gilead (Israelite Transjordan). In 732 B.C.E., Damascus, farther north, and the rest of the land of Syria (Aram) were conquered and then reorganized into an Assyrian province. Before his death in 727 B.C.E., Tiglath-pileser III had reduced Judah, Israel, and Philistia to vassalage and was receiving tribute from the territories of Ammon, Moab, and Edom in Transjordan.

The Last Kings of Israel (746–724 B.C.E.)

After the forty-year reign of Jeroboam II had ended in 746 B.C.E., the Northern Kingdom of Israel experienced a precipitous decline, marking the end of its stability and prosperity. In addition to threats from Assyria and Syria, the kingdom was demoralized by internal power struggles, with intrigues of all kinds, including murder. Jeroboam II was succeeded by his son, Zechariah, whose rule was abruptly terminated after only six months by assassination. Thus ended ingloriously the Jehu dynasty, as Amos and Hosea had predicted. The next king, Shallum, who had murdered Zechariah, was himself killed by his successor, Menahem, after a reign of only one month. Instead of opposing Tiglath-pileser III, Menahem (745–738 B.C.E.) paid him a heavy tribute as a way of currying favor. Pekahiah, the son of Menahem, was pro-Assyrian as was his father; he ruled for only a year before being assassinated by his successor, Pekah. When Pekah (737–732 B.C.E.) took the throne, he advocated an anti-Assyrian policy, which led to the formation of a coalition of Syria (Aram) and Israel against Assyria. It was known as the Syro-Israelite alliance.

Besides Pekah, the other principal organizer of this coalition was Rezin, king of Syria (740–732 B.C.E.). They had the support of Tyre, a leading city of Phoenicia, and Philistia, but Ahaz of Judah refused to join. In an effort to replace Ahaz with the son of a certain Tabeel, the combined forces of Pekah and Rezin attacked Jerusalem, but the venture was unsuccessful.

King Ahaz of Judah (735–715 B.C.E.)

Ahaz, the son of Jotham and the father of Hezekiah, ascended the throne in 735 B.C.E. and ruled for twenty years. Tiglath-pileser III was at the height of his imperial power at that time. The vacillating Ahaz was caught in an impossible bind, between Pekah and Rezin on the one side and Tiglath-pileser III on the other. Apparently, many of Ahaz' subjects favored Judah's participation in the anti-Assyrian coalition of Pekah and Rezin. In desperation he appealed to the Assyrian ruler in order to save his throne. Everyone was a loser except Tiglath-pileser III. In suppressing the anti-Assyrian coalition, he destroyed Damascus and converted the territory of Aram into an Assyrian province; he reduced Israel to the status of Assyrian vassal and made Judah an Assyrian satellite.

The Last Days of Israel

Pekah was murdered by Hoshea, who had the dubious distinction of being the last king of Israel (732–724 B.C.E.). He assumed the throne with the approval of Tiglath-pileser III, to whom he paid a heavy tribute. Sometime after the death of Tiglath-pileser III in 727 B.C.E., Hoshea rebelled, refusing to pay tribute to the Assyrians. Instead, he futilely sought aid from Egypt. Hoshea was imprisoned in 724 B.C.E.; his final fate is unknown.

Shalmaneser V of Assyria (727–722 B.C.E.), son and successor of Tiglath-pileser III, besieged Samaria, which resisted for three years before it fell in 721 B.C.E. His successor, Sargon II (722–705 B.C.E.), did not destroy Samaria but instead deported about thirty thousand citizens, replacing them with foreigners; then he made Samaria an Assyrian province, called Samerina. In effect, this was the end of the Northern Kingdom of Israel. The Southern Kingdom of Judah did not suffer the same fate because of its abiding loyalty to Assyria. In 712 B.C.E., Sargon II laid siege to the Philistine city of Ashdod. Invoking the fate of the Northern Kingdom as a lesson, Micah warned Judah against following the same path: "Therefore I [the LORD] will make Samaria a heap in the open country, a place for planting vineyards; and I will pour down her stones into the valley, and uncover her foundations" (Micah 1:6).

King Hezekiah of Judah (715–687 B.C.E.)

Hezekiah, son of Ahaz, was a vigorous king who addressed religious reform and several other issues, including politics. Enjoying the confidence of priests and prophets, he centralized worship in the Temple of Jerusalem. He also expanded the western boundaries of Jerusalem to accommodate a large influx of people into the capital. Apparently, after the fall of Samaria many refugees from the Northern Kingdom fled to Jerusalem, as well as dispossessed Judahites from the provinces that Sennacherib, son and successor of Sargon II, later took from the Southern Kingdom.

During most of Hezekiah's reign Judah enjoyed great prosperity. Hezekiah's revolt against Assyrian rule at Sargon II's death in 705 B.C.E. was a turning point in the history of Judah. Hezekiah headed a coalition, composed of Phoenicia (the East Mediterranean coastal strip, including modern Syria and Lebanon) and the Philistine cities of Ashkelon and Ekron, against Sennacherib (704–681 B.C.E.), son and successor of Sargon II. Despite the military preparations undertaken by Hezekiah, including the construction of a 1,750-foot tunnel to protect Jerusalem's water supply in the event of an attack, his coalition could not compete against the superior forces of Assyria. In 701 B.C.E., Sennacherib quickly suppressed the revolt in the region to the west of Assyria; he divided some of the territory belonging to the Southern Kingdom of Judah among loyal subjects and reduced Judah to the status of vassal. The tribute exacted of Hezekiah was a serious economic burden on the people. Fortunately, Jerusalem itself was spared destruction when Hezekiah capitulated to Sennacherib.

The Annals of Sennacherib agree substantially with the biblical account (2 Kings 18:13–16): "As for Hezekiah of Judah, who did not submit to my yoke, I laid siege to 46 of his strong cities, walled forts and to the countless small villages in their vicinity, and conquered them. . . . I drove out 200,150 people."

Micah 1:10–15 lists the towns of the Shephelah (the foothills of the central mountain range of Judah), including Lachish, which Sennacherib devastated. The reliefs adorning the walls of Sennacherib's palace at Nineveh on the left bank of the Tigris River provide the most vivid account of his siege and capture of Lachish (see chapter 3). Excavations at some of these sites confirm the violent destruction wrought by the Assyrian army in 701 B.C.E.

Geography in the Eighth Century B.C.E.

Important Cities in the Northern Kingdom

Samaria

The third capital of the Northern Kingdom of Israel, after Shechem and Tirzah, was established at Samaria (Heb.: *shomron*) by King Omri (876–869 B.C.E.). He purchased the site, located about forty-two miles north of Jerusalem, and there built a city. Perched on a hill about three hundred feet above the valley, the site was readily defensible, well located along major trade routes, and within a fertile region cultivated with olive orchards and vineyards. But the city had only a limited water supply, with no springs in the immediate vicinity, and its potential expansion was restricted by the natural contours of the hill.

The eighth-century prophets mention Samaria frequently and always caustically. The Northern Kingdom of Israel, including Samaria, was also called Ephraim, after one of the tribes of Israel. The Northern Kingdom became known as Israel following the secession under Jeroboam I (922–901 B.C.E.) on the occasion of Solomon's death. The modern village at the site of ancient Samaria is named Sebastiyeh, an Arabic corruption of Sebaste (the Greek for "Augustus"), the name conferred by Herod the Great (37–4 B.C.E.) on the city he rebuilt there to honor his patron, the emperor Augustus.

Apart from the work of Frederick Bliss at Tell el-Hesi in 1891 and 1892, Samaria was the first site in Palestine excavated by Americans. Between 1908 and 1910 Harvard University sponsored an expedition led by George Reisner. A second major campaign, under the direction of British archaeologist John Crowfoot, was in the field from 1931 to 1935. The site was extremely difficult to dig; the reuse of stone in the successive rebuilding that took place at Samaria complicated the stratigraphy; also, later construction destroyed earlier phases of occupation. One of the archaeologists commented that working at Samaria was like digging in a quarry.

The archaeologists were able to distinguish six periods of Iron Age occupation at Samaria, from the Israelite settlement in the ninth century B.C.E. to the Assyrian conquest in the eighth, a century and a half later. Fragmentary remains at the site indicate that the Samaria of Omri and his successor Ahab was well built. The royal quarter on the summit was enclosed by beautifully constructed casemate walls (parallel walls joined at intervals by cross walls). James Starkey, British excavator of Lachish, admired the superb craftsmanship of Samaria's inner wall of ashlar masonry (square, dressed stone). Learning from

Crowfoot that it had to be reburied, he wanted to apply for permission to dismantle and rebuild the wall in a London museum, but he was dissuaded.

Among the most valuable artifacts from Samaria are ivory, pottery, and ostraca. More than five hundred fragments of ivory inlays (decorations set into a surface), testimony to the luxury of Samaria, were found in the vicinty of the royal quarter (see chapter 6). Among the pottery vessels found in the ancient Near East, the "Samaria ware"—a term designating the fine burnished (polished) vessels with red slip (veneer) from Samaria—is striking.

Sixty-three ostraca with Hebrew inscriptions in black ink were found, most of them in a building located between the palace of King Omri and a casemate wall in the west. Scholars generally agree that these potsherds date to the time of Jeroboam II in the eighth century B.C.E., but they continue to disagree about the purpose of these ostraca. Some maintain they were tax receipts for the shipment of wine and oil. If so, why would they be left in the storehouse? Some suggest they were records of delivery of wine and oil from neighboring settlements to the royal palace. Others think they were labels affixed to the jars of wine and oil. Whatever their nature, these texts shed light on the language, script, and personal names of the eighth century B.C.E.

The Assyrians rebuilt Samaria, making it the headquarters of the administrative district. In keeping with the Assyrian practice of naming a province after its capital city, the region (the central hill country of Palestine) became known as Samaria (or Samerina), as already pointed out, from the time of the Assyrian conquest. Biblical references predating 721 B.C.E. pertain to the city of Samaria, not to the whole region. After the demise of the Assyrians in 609 B.C.E., Samaria became successively a provincial administrative center of Babylonia and of Persia. After the conquest of Alexander the Great in 332 B.C.E., Samaria became a prosperous Greek city. When Herod rebuilt Samaria (Sebaste) in 30 B.C.E., it attained its greatest splendor.

Hazor

Covering 175 acres, Hazor is located ten miles north of the Sea of Galilee. It was an important commercial center in Canaanite and Israelite times. Joshua destroyed by fire this fortified Canaanite royal city, which is described in the Book of Joshua as "the head of all those kingdoms" (Josh. 11:10). Solomon rebuilt and fortified Hazor as a garrison city, as the Bible records: "This is the account of the forced labor which King Solomon levied to build the house of the LORD and his own house and the Millo and the wall of Jerusalem and Hazor and

Megiddo and Gezer" (1 Kings 9:15). The fortification built by Solomon at Hazor (Stratum X), and also those at Megiddo and Gezer, consisted of a casemate wall and a large gate with six chambers (three on each side), flanked by two towers (see chapter 3).

Israeli archaeologist Yigael Yadin directed the first extensive excavations at Hazor, beginning in 1955. Occupied first in the Early Bronze Age (3300–2000 B.C.E.), the site, composed of an upper and a lower city, had twenty-one strata. The lower city flourished throughout the Middle Bronze Age (2000–1550 B.C.E.) and the Late Bronze Age (1550–1200 B.C.E.). From the time of Solomon onward, only the upper city was occupied. After the eighth century B.C.E., occupation of the site was quite limited.

Stratum VI, dating to Jeroboam II (786–746 B.C.E.), gives evidence of a flourishing city. Especially noteworthy in this period were the Israelite houses; the workmanship of the builders was excellent. The excavators uncovered a four-room house with two stories, the second floor supported by pillars; the stone staircase was also intact (see chapter 3). This prosperous city appears to have been destroyed by an earthquake; the tilted walls of building remains are consistent with an earthquake. This may be the same earthquake mentioned in Amos 1:1. After the earthquake, the city was rebuilt immediately.

The broken vessels lying on the floors amidst ashes in Stratum V are evidence of the destruction by fire wrought at Hazor by Tiglath-pileser III in 732 B.C.E. The inhabitants of the city must have anticipated the Assyrian advance when they undertook to strengthen the citadel with an offset-inset wall (a solid wall with projections and recesses).

Hazor never really recovered, but Stratum IV reveals that after the Assyrian destruction there was an unwalled settlement at Hazor in the eighth to seventh centuries B.C.E.

Megiddo

Megiddo, a Canaanite and Israelite city, overlooks the Valley of Jezreel (Plain of Esdraelon). Megiddo's thirteen-acre site was strategically located from the point of view of military considerations and trade routes; it also had a good water supply. Megiddo was first excavated from 1903 to 1905 by Gottlieb Schumacher; the major expedition to Megiddo was conducted under the auspices of the University of Chicago from 1925 to 1939. In all, twenty strata were distinguished, extending from the early fourth millennium to the Persian period (538–332 B.C.E.).

As an indication of Megiddo's importance, the city is mentioned in several ancient texts, including the Bible and the Amarna Letters, the archives of Pharaoh Amenophis IV of Egypt. Armageddon ("mountain of Megiddo") is mentioned in Rev. 16:16 as the site of the final cosmic battle. According to 1 Kings 9:15, Solomon fortified Megiddo. After the Chicago excavations, however, confusion remained concerning the stratigraphy of the Solomonic period. Attempting to clarify the situation, Yadin made soundings at Megiddo in 1960 and later. He concluded that Strata VA-IVB were Solomonic; Palace 6000 (the earliest Israelite monumental building constructed of ashlar masonry and decorated with Proto-Aeolic [spiral-shaped ornament] stone capitals), the casemate walls, and massive Gate 2156 (constructed of ashlar masonry) with its six chambers and two towers belonged to these levels (see chapter 3). Stratum IVA, including the offset-inset walls, with the four-chamber Gate 500B, the stable compounds (see chapter 6), and the subterranean water system, dated to the Omride dynasty in the first part of the ninth century B.C.E.

Megiddo was a prosperous city in the time of Jeroboam II (786–746 B.C.E.), as the public buildings and storehouses attest. Capturing northern Israel in 733 B.C.E., Tiglath-pileser III made Megiddo the capital of one of the three Assyrian provinces. Stratum III reflects Assyrian influence in the layout of the city and the style of the houses. Gate 500 of this period had only two pairs of piers. The last city, Stratum I, dates from the Persian period (538–332 B.C.E.), when Megiddo was unfortified.

Dan

The traditional formula "from Dan to Beer-sheba" found in 1 Sam. 3:20 and elsewhere describes the northern and southern extremities of ancient Israel. Dan, situated at the foot of Mt. Hermon, is the city on the northern border of Israel. Avraham Biran, who has been excavating this fifty-acre tell since 1966, traces its earliest occupation to the middle of the third millennium. The site continued to be occupied through the Byzantine period (324–640 C.E.).

During both the Canaanite and the Israelite period Dan was surrounded with massive fortifications. A spectacular Canaanite mudbrick gateway consisting of two towers with complete arch, dated to the Middle Bronze II period (1800–1650 B.C.E.), has been uncovered. A gate with fortifications, dating to the time of Jeroboam I (922–901 B.C.E.), has also come to light.

After the schism of the United Kingdom at the death of Solomon in 922 B.C.E., Jeroboam I, the first king of Israel, established two national sanctuaries in the Northern Kingdom, one at Dan and the other at Bethel, by setting up gold bull images in each. The excavator of Dan believes he has unearthed the sacred area, called a *bamah,* or "high place," on the northwest side of the site. An almost square platform (60 × 62 feet), it is thought to have been built by Jeroboam I. Monumental steps were added in the ninth to the eighth century B.C.E., during the reigns of Ahab and Jeroboam II. Cult objects, including incense stands, figurines, and a horned altar, have also been discovered.

Bethel (and Gilgal)

Bethel, situated ten miles north of Jerusalem, was an ancient cult center, associated in the Bible with the patriarch Jacob. Strategically located with respect to water sources and roadways, Bethel was occupied from about 2000 B.C.E. through the Byzantine period (324–640 C.E.). William F. Albright and James Kelso dug at Bethel in 1934; excavations continued during occasional years until 1960.

In Amos' time, Bethel was the chief sanctuary of the Northern Kingdom; it was also a royal sanctuary, where Amaziah was the official priest. Expelling Amos from Bethel, Amaziah said, "It [Bethel] is the king's sanctuary, and it is a temple of the kingdom" (Amos 7:13). Archaeologists have not located the bull sanctuary at this site. The Assyrians apparently destroyed Bethel in 722–721 B.C.E.; later the city was rebuilt.

Amos and Hosea often delivered polemics against Bethel. Hosea contemptuously referred to Bethel ("house of God") as Beth-aven (literally, "house of worthlessness"), a scornful name coined by Amos. Speaking for the Lord, Amos said, "Do not seek Bethel, and do not enter into Gilgal or cross over to Beer-sheba; for Gilgal shall surely go into exile, and Bethel shall come to nought [Heb.: *'aven,* connoting worthlessness]" (Amos 5:5).

The Gilgal ("circle of stones") mentioned in the quotation from Amos cannot be located with certainty, because the name Gilgal was attached to several sites. The prophet apparently is referring to the Gilgal identified with Khirbet (ruin) Mefjir, a mile from Old Testament Jericho (Tell es-Sultan), the site of the first encampment of the Israelites after they crossed the Jordan River.

According to the Book of Joshua: "The people came up out of the Jordan on the tenth day of the first month, and they encamped in Gilgal on the east border of Jericho. And those twelve stones, which they took out of the Jordan, Joshua set up in Gilgal" (Josh. 4:19–20).

On the basis of context, Khirbet Mefjir would seem to be the Gilgal intended by Micah when he reminds the people of God's saving acts on behalf of Israel in the past, beginning with the exodus and continuing with the conquest of Canaan. The text of Micah is defective: "What happened from Shittim to Gilgal" (Micah 6:5), but it appears to refer to the crossing of the Jordan. Shittim was the camp of Israel east of the Jordan, and Gilgal was the encampment on the west side. Surveys in the vicinity of Khirbet Mefjir (Gilgal) revealed that this site had been occupied during the Iron Age (1200–586 B.C.E.).

Warning against pilgrimages to the principal shrines in Israel, Hosea said, "Enter not into Gilgal, nor go up to Beth-aven, and swear not, 'As the LORD lives' " (Hos. 4:15).

At the time of the Syro-Israelite war (735–734 B.C.E.), Judah was intent upon invading the Northern Kingdom of Israel to regain the frontier cities of Gibeah and Ramah. Hosea sounded the cry of alarm: "Blow the horn in Gibeah, the trumpet in Ramah. Sound the alarm at Beth-aven; tremble, O Benjamin!" (Hos. 5:8).

Hosea indicted the cult practiced at the bull sanctuary of Bethel: "The inhabitants of Samaria tremble for the calf of Beth-aven. Its people shall mourn for it, and its idolatrous priests shall wail over it, over its glory which has departed from it" (Hos. 10:5).

Amos quoted the Lord's menacing words against the cult practiced at Bethel: "On the day I punish Israel for his transgressions, I will punish the altars of Bethel, and the horns of the altar shall be cut off and fall to the ground" (Amos 3:14).

Amos also quoted the Lord's cynical invitation to visit the principal sanctuaries of the Northern Kingdom: "Come to Bethel, and transgress; to Gilgal, and multiply transgression; bring your sacrifices every morning, your tithes every three days" (Amos 4:4).

Important Cities in the Southern Kingdom

Jerusalem

Isaiah 52:1 refers to Jerusalem as "the holy city," and it continues to be sacred to three major religions: Judaism, Christianity, and Islam. From the third millennium until the tenth century B.C.E., settlement was limited to the Ophel Hill (City of David), which extended south from today's Dome of the Rock (Temple Mount) and is outside the present walls of the Old City. Two considerations made the southern spur an ideal location for the earliest city: proximity to water from the perennial Gihon spring, and natural defense by deep valleys on three sides.

David (1000–961 B.C.E.) captured Jerusalem from the Jebusites and made it the royal and religious capital of the nation. Solomon (961–922 B.C.E.) built the palace and the Temple, and he extended the city's walls in a northerly direction to enclose the Temple Mount. In response to the threat of invasion, several later kings of Judah fortified the capital or refurbished it after destruction.

Hezekiah's contribution to Jerusalem was notable. In preparation for the Assyrian siege under Sennacherib in 701 B.C.E., he took steps necessary to protect Jerusalem's water supply. He constructed a water tunnel through bedrock to carry water from the vulnerable Gihon spring, located outside the city wall on the east side of the city, to the Siloam pool on the southwest side of the city. The details surrounding this engineering feat are well known from the "Siloam inscription" carved on the east wall of the tunnel. Found in 1880, it describes the undertaking in detail. The tunnel, 1,750 feet long, was cut through bedrock by two teams of laborers; digging from opposite directions through the solid rock, they eventually met.

Hezekiah also strengthened the city walls. With the influx of refugees, the population reached twenty-five thousand; the city was able to accommodate the increased number by expanding westward to include a residential quarter called the Mishneh ("second quarter") and the Machtesh ("mortar"). These two sections of Jerusalem are mentioned in Zeph. 1:10–11 and elsewhere, but little is known about them. The western hill is also called the Upper City, distinguished from the Lower City which includes the City of David and the Temple Mount.

According to Nahman Avigad, excavator of the Jewish Quarter in the Old City of Jerusalem, as early as the eighth century B.C.E. people were living on the western ridge of Jerusalem, the area that may have been known as the Mishneh and the Machtesh. A segment of the massive stone wall surrounding the western ridge was uncovered during recent excavations; it measured 22 feet thick and 10 feet high. It probably was constructed by Hezekiah to protect the western hill from Assyrian invaders.

Despite the prominence of Jerusalem in both history and religion, the city was practically unknown archaeologically until the nineteenth century. In 1865, when the Palestine Exploration Fund was established in London, the British began the archaeological investigation of Jerusalem. Charles Warren made a great contribution to the topography of Jerusalem by tracing the lines of the city walls and of the Temple Mount.

Since 1967, Israeli archaeologists have been excavating intensively in Jerusalem; as already indicated, three projects stand out. Benjamin Mazar, working adjacent to the retaining walls of the Temple Mount, concentrated on the area south and southwest of the temenos (sacred precinct). Avigad excavated in the center of the Jewish Quarter (the

Upper City) and established that in the eighth century B.C.E. Jerusalem was not limited to the narrow City of David but it also incorporated the western hill. Yigal Shiloh, continuing the work of British archaeologist Kathleen Kenyon, excavated the City of David, southeast of the Temple Mount. There he unearthed twenty-five occupational strata, extending from the Chalcolithic period (4200–3300 B.C.E.) to medieval times. Shiloh's excavations in the City of David have clarified, among other considerations, the three interconnected water installations of the Iron Age, all fed by the Gihon spring. In addition to Hezekiah's tunnel were the Siloam channel and "Warren's Shaft," so called after Charles Warren, who discovered in 1867 a vertical shaft with connecting tunnels which gave the residents of Jerusalem access to the waters of the Gihon spring.

Jerusalem's principal importance is as a theological symbol, summed up in the term "Zion tradition," which is based on the bringing of the Ark of the Covenant to Jerusalem and the building of the Temple. With David's transfer of the Ark to Jerusalem, Mt. Zion (Jerusalem) became the Lord's chosen mountain. Although topographically a low hill, Jerusalem was considered in the Zion tradition to be a lofty mountain. To pay tribute to the Lord, the nations were to make pilgrimages to Jerusalem.

The exaltation of Jerusalem, prophesied by Micah and by Isaiah (Isa. 2:2–3), is described in a well-known passage, which incorporates several elements of the Zion tradition:

> It shall come to pass in the latter days that the mountain of the house of the LORD shall be established as the highest of the mountains, and shall be raised up above the hills; and peoples shall flow to it, and many nations shall come, and say: "Come, let us go up to the mountain of the LORD, to the house of the God of Jacob; that he may teach us his ways and we may walk in his paths." For out of Zion shall go forth the law, and the word of the LORD from Jerusalem. (Micah 4:1–2)

A central feature of the Zion tradition is belief in the inviolability of Jerusalem. The fact of Jerusalem's deliverance from Sennacherib in 701 B.C.E. reinforced this aspect of the Zion tradition. Micah, however, denounced Judah's confidence in the inviolability of Zion, asserting that Jerusalem and the Temple would be destroyed: "Therefore because of you Zion shall be plowed as a field; Jerusalem shall become a heap of ruins, and the mountain of the house a wooded height" (Micah 3:12). A century later when Jeremiah was threatened with death for his "Temple sermon" which the religious authorities interpreted as blasphemous, Micah's words were recalled in the prophet's defense

(Jer. 26:18). The contrast between this audacious statement of Micah and his prophecy about Jerusalem's exaltation makes it hard to believe the two were uttered by the same person. Apparently, the one is an indictment of prevailing conditions, the other a vision of future glory.

Lachish

The most important city in Judah after Jerusalem was Lachish, situated twenty-five miles southwest of Jerusalem in the Judean hills. First settled in the middle of the fourth millennium, Lachish was a large Canaanite city-state in the Late Bronze Age (1550–1200 B.C.E.). It suffered a major destruction in the twelfth century B.C.E., which may be attributed to the Israelite attack under Joshua. When the United Kingdom was split at the death of Solomon, Lachish was rebuilt and became a garrison city. After having been destroyed by the Assyrians and later the Babylonians, Lachish was reconstructed and then occupied during the Persian and Hellenistic periods.

Excavations at Lachish were first conducted from 1932 to 1938 by British archaeologist James Starkey. The next major excavation began in 1973 under the direction of Israeli archaeologist David Ussishkin; it is still in progress. Building on the results of his predecessor, Ussishkin has unraveled a major problem concerning the date of the destruction of Stratum III at Lachish.

During Hezekiah's prosperous reign Lachish was a garrison city, fortified by two massive city walls. The city gate, the largest known from the Israelite period, was near the southwest corner of the tell, the most accessible and thereby the most vulnerable part of the city; the remaining sides were protected by deep valleys. A large palace-fortress commanded the center of the city (see chapter 3). Lachish needed all the defenses it could muster when Sennacherib ascended the throne of Assyria in 704 B.C.E. The alliance that Egypt, some of the Philistine city-states, and Judah forged against Assyria provoked Sennacherib to action. His attack against Lachish focused on the vulnerable southwest corner. When the Assyrians built a siege ramp of earth and stone against this southwest corner of the city wall, the Judahite defenders responded by constructing a counterramp opposite the Assyrian siege ramp. The destruction wrought by the Assyrians under Sennacherib is reflected in Stratum III, dating to 701 B.C.E.

Micah lists Lachish among the Judahite cities destroyed by Sennacherib (Micah 1:13). According to the Annals of Sennacherib, forty-six of Hezekiah's fortified cities were conquered. The details of the attack and its aftermath are documented on the palace reliefs of Sennacherib at Nineveh, his capital. They are a rich source of information on for-

The city of Lachish. Judith Dekel's reconstruction of Lachish as it appeared in the late eighth century B.C.E. is based on recent excavations at the site. The city had a double fortification wall and a double gateway. The palace-fortress was situated in the center of the city. (*Courtesy of the Expedition to Lachish, David Ussishkin, Director; drawing by Judith Dekel*)

tifications and warfare in the eighth century B.C.E. (see chapter 3). An inscription accompanying the Assyrian reliefs makes it clear that Lachish was the city under siege.

Lachish was destroyed again in 588/586 B.C.E., this time by the Babylonians, who also made the vulnerable southwest corner of the city the object of their attack. This siege, reflected in Stratum II, is well documented by twenty-one Hebrew inscriptions (the Lachish Letters), in the form of an exchange of letters between two military commanders. Most of these ostraca were discovered in a guardroom of the outer gate of the double-gate complex at Lachish.

Arad

Arad, situated in the eastern Negev about eighteen miles northeast of Beer-sheba, is composed of two settlements. The lower city of more than twenty-nine acres flourished in the Early Bronze Age II (3000–2800 B.C.E.); the upper mound or acropolis was the site of six successive Israelite fortresses in Iron Age II (1000–586 B.C.E.), each destroyed apparently by sudden attack, according to the excavator Yohanan Aharoni. In all, twelve strata were distinguished on the upper mound. The site appears not to have been occupied in the Middle and Late Bronze Ages; consequently it cannot be identified with Canaanite Arad, if the biblical tradition concerning the Canaanite city is to be accepted. On the other hand, there is inscriptional evidence to support the identification of Tel Arad with Israelite Arad. Israeli archaeologists began excavation in Arad in 1962; Ruth Amiran directed the dig at the Early Bronze Age city, while Aharoni concentrated on the Iron Age fortress.

In the Israelite period Arad was an important frontier fortress, guarding the eastern Negev. The earlier fortresses, a little larger than the later ones, measured about 165 × 180 feet. Associated with the earlier fortresses was an Israelite sanctuary in the northwest corner; it followed a broad-room plan of construction with the entrance on the long side (in contrast to the Jerusalem Temple's long-room plan) and was complete with sacrificial altar, the "holy of holies" (*adytum*), and cultic objects. Two incense altars of stone were found on the steps leading to the "holy of holies" (see chapter 4). The citadels and associated sanctuaries at Arad would have served as both religious and administrative centers on the southern border of the Kingdom of Judah. The Arad sanctuary is reminiscent of "the king's sanctuary" at Bethel, from which Amos was expelled by the priest Amaziah (Amos 7:13).

Dating Strata IX and VIII to the eighth century B.C.E., Aharoni conjectured that Stratum IX was destroyed by an Edomite raid during the Syro-Israelite war in 734 B.C.E., and he attributed the destruction of Stratum VIII to Sennacherib in 701 B.C.E.

About two hundred ostraca from the royal archives were found at Arad. Half were inscribed in Aramaic and date to 400 B.C.E.; the remainder were in Hebrew and date to the Iron Age.

Beer-sheba

Well known from the traditional description of the Israelite borders, "from Dan [in the north] to Beer-sheba [in the south]," dating from the time of King David (1000–961 B.C.E.), Beer-sheba was the principal city of the northern Negev. In the Israelite period it was an administrative and military center.

Excavations began at Beer-sheba in 1969 under Aharoni and continued through 1976. The city was quite small, only three acres in area. Situated about four miles from the modern city of Beer-sheba, Tel Beer-sheba was composed of five occupational levels, dating to the Israelite period (Iron Age). Occupation at Beer-sheba was short-lived, lasting only about two hundred and fifty years; apparently the city was destroyed in 701 B.C.E. by Sennacherib.

Two features of Beer-sheba stand out: its fortifications and its city planning. It had a strong fortification system. Casemate walls were constructed in the ninth century B.C.E. (Stratum III) and continued in use through the eighth century B.C.E., until they were destroyed by fire at the end of that century (Stratum II). Beer-sheba was a carefully planned administrative city. According to Aharoni, it is the first example of a planned city from the time of the monarchy. A street, with buildings on each side, encircled the city. The excavator also mentions four-room houses at Beer-sheba (they appear on the plans to be three-room houses); this type of house usually consisted of one broad room and three long rooms divided by rows of pillars. The remnants of stairs indicate that these houses had two stories. Several public buildings were unearthed in the vicinity of the gate. Each of the three adjoining buildings to the right of the gate consisted of three long halls, separated by two rows of pillars. The excavators identified these structures as storehouses, but some others think they were stables as at Megiddo.

Beer-sheba received no accolades from Amos, who was extremely critical of the worshipers' cultic practices there. The fact that Amos indicts the sanctuary at Beer-sheba at the same time that he passes judgment on the shrines at Dan, Bethel, Gilgal, and Samaria suggests that Beer-sheba was among the most prominent places of worship in the eighth century B.C.E. Beer-sheba was a venerable shrine, tracing its history as a sacred site to the patriarchs Abraham, Isaac, and Jacob. The date of the patriarchal age is a perennial problem, which has not yet been solved satisfactorily. The question must be asked whether Tel Beer-sheba is the site of the ancient patriarchal city. Although Aharoni concentrated on Iron Age II (1000–586 B.C.E.), there was indication at the site of "a modest village" for two centuries earlier. If the patriarchal age were to date so late (1200–1000 B.C.E.), such would be the evidence for the patriarchs at Beer-sheba.

Once again Amos quotes the Lord's words of denunciation to Israel: "Those who swear by Ashimah of Samaria, and say, 'As thy god lives, O Dan,' and, 'As the way of Beer-sheba lives,' they shall fall, and never rise again" (Amos 8:14). "Ashimah" may designate the goddess of the settlers of Hamath in Syria who practiced her cult in Samaria after 722 B.C.E. (see chapter 4). "As the way of Beer-sheba lives" is enigmatic, but it may refer to a pilgrimage route leading to the sanctuary at Beer-sheba.

Mizpah

The evidence is not definitive, but Tell en-Nasbeh, eight miles north of Jerusalem, is generally identified with Mizpah of Benjamin. The seven-acre tell, situated on the border of Judah and Israel, was occupied almost continuously from 1100 until the fourth century B.C.E. Surrounded by deep valleys on three sides, the site is strategically located. Owing to its location and massive fortifications, it may have served as the boundary fortress between the Kingdoms of Judah and Israel. Tell en-Nasbeh was the first Palestinian site to be dug completely when William Badè directed five campaigns there from 1926 to 1935.

The great city wall deserves special mention; it was the offset-inset type, enhanced by ten towers. Forty feet high and 16 feet thick, the wall was protected by a glacis (sloping ramp) as well as by a fosse (ditch) which ran along sections of the outside of the wall. A well-preserved gateway with two pairs of piers was also uncovered. Soldiers approaching the gate from the east had to make a left turn, thus exposing their vulnerable right side (see chapter 3).

Tell en-Nasbeh was also a well-planned city, and the four-room house was typical of the more prominent buildings. Rectangular in shape, three rooms formed a square, and a fourth was situated along the width of the dwelling. Many would maintain that the middle of the three parallel rooms was an open central courtyard. Lawrence Stager argues convincingly, however, that these houses were completely roofed, and some had an upper story (see chapter 3).

In an indictment of Israel's leaders, Hosea states: "Hear this, O priests! Give heed, O house of Israel! Hearken, O house of the king! For the judgment pertains to you; for you have been a snare at Mizpah, and a net spread upon Tabor" (Hos. 5:1). Sometimes the references of Hosea and the prophets are so cryptic that they elude modern commentators. As at many sites, figurines of Astarte, the Canaanite goddess of fertility, were found at Mizpah; Hosea may have been alluding to the practice of fertility cults there.

Amos' Oracles Against the Nations

According to the theology of Amos, God's sovereignty is universal; extending far beyond Israel and Judah, the Lord's sphere is international. The Book of Amos begins (1:3–2:16) with eight oracles of judgment against the nations of Syria-Palestine, the immediate neighbors of Israel and Judah, most of whom were part of the Davidic empire and hence obligated by the treaty (covenant) over which the Lord presided. These announcements of judgments may have been delivered by Amos at one of the festivals when a large crowd of the people would have been assembled. There may be a deliberate geographical order in the presentation of these indictments: the prophet begins in the northeast with Aram (Syria), moves to the southwest with Philistia, then to the northwest with Tyre, and ends in the southeast with Edom, Ammon, and Moab. Owing to the time span separating Amos and the modern reader, it is impossible to identify all the events to which he alludes in these oracles.

Against Damascus

> Thus says the LORD: "For three transgressions of Damascus, and for four, I will not revoke the punishment; because they have threshed Gilead with threshing sledges of iron. So I will send a fire upon the house of Hazael, and it shall devour the strongholds of Ben-hadad. I will break the bar of Damascus, and cut off the inhabitants from the Valley of Aven, and him that holds the scepter from Beth-eden; and the people of Syria shall go into exile to Kir," says the LORD. (Amos 1:3–5)

Beginning in the middle of the ninth century B.C.E., border wars between Aram and Israel were common for about a century. Aram of the Old Testament (modern Syria) was a confederation of states in the dual role of Israel's neighbors and rivals during the period of the monarchy (Iron Age II). The Aramean states were eventually assimilated into the Assyrian provinces. Damascus, capital of modern

Syria, was the center of Aramean power and religion. Situated in an oasis, Damascus was at the crossroads of the military and commercial routes throughout the ancient Near East.

David had defeated Damascus and made Aram a tributary of his kingdom. Later, to arrest the imperial ambitions of Assyrian king Shalmaneser III (859–825 B.C.E.), Ben-hadad of Damascus and Ahab of Israel formed a coalition and confronted him at Qarqar (north of Damascus) in 853 B.C.E. In the days of the Jehu dynasty of Israel, King Hazael (842–806 B.C.E.) of Damascus campaigned against Israel, conquering its Transjordanian territory. Another Ben-hadad (a throne name used by successive kings of Aram), son and successor of Hazael, captured some cities from Israel during the reign of Jehoahaz (815–801 B.C.E.), until his son Joash (801–786 B.C.E.) succeeded in recapturing them. Later, Jeroboam II was victorious over Damascus. The kingdom of Aram met its demise in 732 B.C.E. when overrun by Tiglath-pileser III in retaliation for the Syro-Israelite alliance against Assyria, perpetrated by Rezin of Damascus and Pekah of Israel.

Gilead, a highland region in Transjordan, is bounded on the north by the Yarmuk River and on the south by the city of Heshbon. The land of Gilead has always been famous for its fertile land; for that reason Micah was able to say, "Let them feed in Bashan [a fertile plateau adjacent to Gilead] and Gilead as in the days of old" (Micah 7:14). The King's Highway ("the royal way"), the well-known international caravan roadway in Transjordan extending from Damascus to the Gulf of Aqaba, passed through Gilead. Control over Gilead alternated between Israel and Aram, until it was taken by Tiglath-pileser III in 734 B.C.E. In his oracle against Aram, Amos refers to the devastation of Gilead at the hands of Aram's King Hazael.

Hosea makes a serious charge against Gilead, when he says, "Gilead is a city of evildoers, tracked with blood" (Hos. 6:8). The vagueness of the accusation makes it impossible to identify the historical reference behind the verse.

In another obscure verse Hosea, paralleling Gilead and Gilgal, indicts Gilead for illicit cultic practices: "If there is iniquity in Gilead they shall surely come to nought" (Hos. 12:11).

In his indictment against Aram, Amos mentions the Valley of Aven and Beth-eden. Concerning the first reference, inasmuch as Hosea was inclined to use Beth-aven as a nickname for Bethel, Aven may refer specifically to Bethel. Hosea states: "The high places of Aven [wickedness], the sin of Israel, shall be destroyed" (Hos. 10:8). Amos may be using the "Valley of Aven" in the figurative sense, with reference to the bull sanctuaries erected at Dan and Bethel by Jeroboam I.

The connotation of Beth-eden ("house of pleasure") is also somewhat obscure. Abraham Malamat convincingly identifies it with Bit-Adini, the Aramean state on the banks of the middle Euphrates River. Founded in the tenth century B.C.E., Bit-Adini was conquered in 855 B.C.E. by Assyrian king Shalmaneser III, when it became an Assyrian province. Malamat argues that at the time of Amos, Bit-Adini was ruled by Shamshi-ilu, an Assyrian noble, to whom Amos refers as "him that holds the scepter from Beth-eden" (Amos 1:5).

Kir was in Mesopotamia, but its precise location is unknown. It was the place of origin of the Arameans, as Amos, quoting the Lord, attests: "Did I not bring up Israel from the land of Egypt, and the Philistines from Caphtor [Crete] and the Syrians [Arameans] from Kir?" (Amos 9:7). The Arameans' punishment would take the form of exile to Kir as a consequence of the Assyrian policy of deportation.

Against Philistia

> Thus says the LORD: "For three transgressions of Gaza, and for four, I will not revoke the punishment; because they carried into exile a whole people to deliver them up to Edom. So I will send a fire upon the wall of Gaza, and it shall devour her strongholds. I will cut off the inhabitants from Ashdod, and him that holds the scepter from Ashkelon; I will turn my hand against Ekron; and the remnant of the Philistines shall perish," says the Lord GOD. (Amos 1:6–8)

Four of the five Philistine cities (Gaza, Ashdod, Ashkelon, and Ekron; Amos does not list Gath here but refers to "Gath of the Philistines" in Amos 6:2) are indicted for their slave traffic with Edom in Transjordan. The Sea Peoples, including the Philistines, first appeared in the East Mediterranean basin after 1180/1175 B.C.E. Migrating from the Aegean Sea, situated between the Greek peninsula on the west and Asia Minor on the east, they settled on the southern coast of Canaan (the ancient name for Palestine) between modern Tel Aviv (in the north) and Gaza (in the south). According to Amos, as just mentioned, the Philistines came from Caphtor (the Hebrew name for Crete): "Did I not bring up Israel from the land of Egypt, and the Philistines from Caphtor [Crete] and the Syrians from Kir?" (Amos 9:7). The designation "Palestine" derives from *Palaistinoi,* the Greek name for the descendants of the Philistines. (Palestine was revived as an official title after World War I.) The Philistines attacked Syria, Palestine, and Egypt, before being defeated by Pharaoh Rameses III of Egypt in 1175 B.C.E. Then they settled along the southern coastal plain of Canaan.

Competing for the same territory, the Philistines and the Israelites became fierce rivals. King David (1000–961 B.C.E.) defeated the Philistines, but that did not put an end to the fighting, which continued intermittently through the ninth century B.C.E.; the eighth century also witnessed intense hostilities between Philistia and Judah. Ahaz of Judah was forced to sacrifice territory to the Philistines, but Hezekiah, his son, apparently was more successful against them. From 735 B.C.E. until the demise of the Southern Kingdom of Judah in 586 B.C.E., the Philistines were dominated by the Assyrians, then later by the Babylonians. In 701 B.C.E., Sennacherib captured Ashkelon; in 609 B.C.E. the Babylonian king Nebuchadnezzar destroyed Ashkelon. However, the Philistine kings, generally loyal vassals of Assyria, enjoyed some limited autonomy because they acted as buffers between Egypt and Assyria.

Almost nothing is known about the Philistine language because of the lack of written records, although there are a few as yet undeciphered inscriptions. Archaeology is shedding some light through excavation of the Philistine Pentapolis ("five cities") and of other sites such as Tel Qasile on the outskirts of modern Tel Aviv, which may prove to be the most important site for learning about the Philistines and their culture. Excavator Amihai Mazar uncovered three superimposed Philistine temples at Tel Qasile; this is the first time a Philistine temple has come to light. Also, many cultic vessels were discovered in the various buildings.

The Philistines have been the victims of a bad press throughout history. Even in modern parlance, "Philistine" is used inaccurately as a synonym for barbarian or ignoramus. In fact, Philistines contributed significantly to the arts, architecture, pottery, crafts, and metallurgy of the area they settled. Also, there is archaeological evidence that under the influence of their neighbors the Philistines adopted the local culture.

Gaza

Amos condemns Gaza for its slave trade with Edom. The southernmost city of the Philistine Pentapolis, Gaza is about three miles from the Mediterranean coast. Modern Tell Harube is identified as the site of ancient Gaza. No significant excavation of the tell has been undertaken, because the ancient city is buried under the modern one. It was only partially excavated by W. J. Phythian-Adams in 1922. Apparently the site was occupied continuously from the Late Bronze Age (1550–1200 B.C.E.) until the Byzantine period (324–640 C.E.).

Gaza figures prominently in the Samson saga; the well-known Philistine temple of Dagon was located there. Tiglath-pileser III captured Gaza, but it remained a Philistine city. Hezekiah also conquered Gaza (2 Kings 18:8), but he was unable to retain it. When Judah rebelled

against Sennacherib during the reign of Hezekiah, some of the Judahite territory was given to Gaza for its loyalty to Assyria.

Ashdod

Known as Azotus in the Hellenistic and Roman periods, Ashdod is
situated three miles inland and ten miles north of Ashkelon. It is a
large site: twenty acres on the acropolis and seventy acres in the lower
city. Moshe Dothan excavated Ashdod from 1962 to 1972. Founded in
the Middle Bronze Age II (1800–1650 B.C.E.), Ashdod was one of the
largest cities in Palestine in Iron Age I (1200–1000 B.C.E.). Ashdod was
distinctively Philistine, according to the excavators, in the twelfth and
eleventh centuries B.C.E. Later, in Iron Age II, Ashdod's gate and
towers were similar in plan to those of Gezer, Megiddo, and Hazor; all
other evidence indicates that it was still a Philistine city.

King Uzziah of Judah (783–742 B.C.E.) conquered Ashdod and adjacent territory. As the result of a revolt against Sargon II of Assyria
(722–705 B.C.E.), Ashdod and Gath were conquered by the Assyrians,
who converted their territory into an Assyrian province. Having remained loyal to Sennacherib in his campaign of 701 B.C.E. against
Phoenicia, Philistia, and Judah, Ashdod received some of Judah's land.

Ashkelon

The history of Ashkelon (from which "scallion" is derived) extends
from 2000 B.C.E. to 1500 C.E. The only Philistine city situated on the
coast, Ashkelon was one of the most important seaports in the East
Mediterranean. Ashkelon is mentioned for the first time in the Execra-
tion Texts (containing curses by pharaohs against their enemies) of the
Middle Kingdom of Egypt, dating to 1850 B.C.E. The principal mound
measures twelve acres; today it is a national park of Israel. Ashkelon
of the Byzantine and Islamic eras included about 150 acres. In a sense,
it can be said that the first excavation in Palestine took place at Ashkelon when British Lady Hester Stanhope went to the site in 1815 and
unearthed statuary. In the process a huge statue of a Roman emperor
was smashed. From 1920 to 1922 British archaeologists John Garstang
and Phythian-Adams undertook limited excavations. The first major
expedition to Ashkelon, under the direction of Stager, began in 1985;
this long-term project will be in the field for several years.

On the temple wall at Karnak in Upper Egypt is depicted the siege
of Ashkelon by the armies of the Egyptians. The victory, traditionally
attributed to Pharaoh Rameses II, has been redated to the reign of
Merenptah, successor of Rameses II, in 1207 B.C.E. Tiglath-pileser III
invaded Ashkelon in 734 B.C.E. For the next twenty-five years, Ashkelon was spared by not participating in the rebellions of the neighboring

Philistine cities. Later, in 701 B.C.E., Sennacherib conquered Ashkelon. In summary, during the eighth and seventh centuries B.C.E. Ashkelon was conquered successively by Assyria, Egypt, and Babylonia.

Ekron

The northernmost city of the Philistine Pentapolis, Ekron is almost certainly located at Tel Miqne, ten miles inland from Ashdod and twenty-two miles west of Jerusalem. Tel Miqne, measuring more than fifty acres, is one of the largest Iron Age sites in Israel; it is also situated in a fertile area with a more than adequate water supply. The first major excavation of the mound began in 1984 under the codirectorship of Trude Dothan and Seymour Gitin.

From about 1200 to 600 B.C.E., Ekron was an important Philistine political and commercial center. Assyrian King Sargon II conquered Ekron in 712 B.C.E., as depicted on Assyrian reliefs at Khorsabad (in northern Iraq) and mentioned in Assyrian historical records.

In Sennacherib's campaign against Judah in 701 B.C.E., Padi, the king of Ekron, remained loyal to Assyria, refusing to join Hezekiah's rebellion. As a result, Hezekiah imprisoned Padi. However, Sennacherib had him restored to power in Ekron and ceded to him some of the land seized from Judah. Ekron remained a Philistine city until the end of the seventh century B.C.E. As part of the Babylonian conquest, Nebuchadnezzar destroyed Ekron in 603 B.C.E., when it ceased to be a significant city.

One of the most important olive oil production centers in the ancient Near East, Ekron reached the height of its economic activity in the late seventh century B.C.E. To date, over one hundred olive oil press installations have been uncovered at Ekron. They are equipped with a large crushing basin and are flanked on each side by a press (see chapter 6). Oil was an important commodity in international trade during the Iron Age, with the import of olives from Judah and the export of oil through the Philistine port cities. A number of incense altars were also found among the oil installations at Ekron.

Against Tyre

> Thus says the LORD: "For three transgressions of Tyre, and for four, I will not revoke the punishment; because they delivered up a whole people to Edom, and did not remember the covenant of brotherhood. So I will send a fire upon the wall of Tyre, and it shall devour her strongholds." (Amos 1:9–10)

The geographical term "Phoenicia," dating from the Iron Age, is a Greek translation of "Canaan." It is conjectured that both names mean "purple dye," extracted from crushed mollusks for which the region was famous. In antiquity Phoenicia was the designation of the coastal strip where Syria and Lebanon are located today; it extended from Arvad in the north to Acco in the south. Phoenicia was organized into independent city-states, including Tyre, Sidon, Arvad, Byblos, and Ugarit. Taking advantage of a number of natural harbors in their region, the Phoenicians were seafarers, engaging in trade and colonization; they were also superb craftsmen. Politically and culturally the Phoenicians maintained a close relationship with Israel in the Iron Age. This relationship was reinforced by political marriage, notably when Jezebel, a Phoenician princess, married King Ahab of Israel (869–850 B.C.E.). Their daughter Athaliah in turn married King Jehoram of Judah. Both Jezebel and Athaliah eagerly promoted the religion of Phoenicia in Israel and Judah. The Phoenicians' deity was Baal, the principal rival in Canaan of Yahweh, the God of Israel; Baal's consort was Astarte. There was no room in Israel for both Yahweh and Baal, as the prophet Elijah made plain. When Jehu (842–815 B.C.E.), the exterminator of the house of Ahab, killed Jezebel by having her pushed out of the palace window and trampled by horses and chariots (2 Kings 9:30–37), diplomatic relations between Phoenicia and Israel deteriorated. Jehu resented the introduction of Phoenician religious practices into the Northern Kingdom, but that could hardly justify his bloody coup.

With the ascent of Tiglath-pileser III to the throne of Assyria in 745 B.C.E., the Phoenicians began to decline. Later, Sennacherib (704–681 B.C.E.) attacked Phoenicia, capturing much of the Phoenician mainland; he also set up a new king, Ethbaal, in Sidon.

Tyre, originally an island but connected with the mainland from the time of Alexander the Great (336–323 B.C.E.), was an important Phoenician city during the first millennium B.C.E. Ancient Tyre consisted of two cities: the island city and the mainland. King Hiram of Tyre (981–947 B.C.E.) is celebrated in the Bible for having supplied David and Solomon with cedar, pine, and craftsmen for various building projects, including the Temple. Assaulted successively by Assyria, Babylonia, and Persia, Tyre was reduced to a minor port after Alexander's conquest in 332 B.C.E.

Against Edom

> Thus says the LORD: "For three transgressions of Edom, and for four, I will not revoke the punishment; because he pursued his brother with the sword, and cast off all pity, and his anger tore perpetually, and he kept his wrath for ever. So I will send a fire

upon Teman, and it shall devour the strongholds of Bozrah."
(Amos 1:11–12)

Edom is the rugged region located south of the Dead Sea on both
sides of the Wadi Arabah. The name "Edom" means "the red region,"
derived from the reddish sandstone found in the region. Edom is
separated from Moab on the north by the Brook Zered (Wadi el-Hesa).
The King's Highway ran north–south through the middle of Edom; the
prosperity of Edom was derived from control over the caravan routes
passing from India and South Arabia to Egypt.

According to Amos, Edom engaged in slave trade with the Philistines (Amos 1:6) and Tyre (1:9). Little is known about Edom, because
no major inscriptions have yet come to light. David (1000–961 B.C.E.)
succeeded in conquering the Edomites. During the reign of Jehoram
of Judah (849–842 B.C.E.), the Edomites revolted and then were able
to maintain independence for about sixty years. From the eighth century B.C.E., Edom was a significant kingdom. Uzziah of Judah recap-
tured Edom, but in the reign of Ahaz, Edom defeated Judah. Edom
paid tribute to Tiglath-pileser III of Assyria (745–727 B.C.E.), and for
the next hundred years Edom was a vassal to Assyria. During the
conquest of Judah in 586 B.C.E., the Edomites helped the Babylonians
sack Jerusalem (Ps. 137:7). After the fall of Jerusalem, the Edomites
migrated west of the Wadi Arabah to southern Judah, where they
became the Idumeans of the Hellenistic and Early Roman periods.
Then the Nabateans, an Arab people of uncertain origin, replaced the
Edomites in Transjordan, making Petra, the famous city cut into rose-
colored rock southeast of the Dead Sea, their capital.

In his indictment of Edom, Amos mentions two principal cities:
Teman in the south and Bozrah in the north. Perhaps Teman was not
a specific site but may refer to southern Edom. There is, however, a
modern village near Petra, named Tawilan, with remains from a large,
unfortified agricultural settlement, dating to the Iron II period (1000–
586 B.C.E.).

Bozrah (modern Buseirah) may mean "fortified place" or "sheep-
fold." Located thirty-five miles north of Petra, it was an important
fortress city. Beginning in 1971, this site was dug for a decade by
British archaeologist Crystal-Margaret Bennett, who reported that the
eighth century B.C.E. marked the major period of occupation at Buseirah. This nineteen-acre site was extremely well fortified; in addition to
its natural defenses formed by deep ravines, the city was surrounded
by a wall thirteen feet wide. In his indictment of Edom, Amos apparently has these major defenses in mind when he speaks of "the strong-

holds of Bozrah" (Amos, 1:12). The acropolis of the city was surrounded by houses typical of the Iron II period.

Against Ammon

> Thus says the LORD: "For three transgressions of the Ammonites, and for four, I will not revoke the punishment; because they have ripped up women with child in Gilead, that they might enlarge their border. So I will kindle a fire in the wall of Rabbah, and it shall devour her strongholds, with shouting in the day of battle, with a tempest in the day of the whirlwind; and their king shall go into exile, he and his princes together," says the LORD. (Amos 1:13–15)

Living north of the Edomites and the Moabites, the Ammonites were situated in north-central Transjordan. Rabbah, their capital, was located at the site of modern Amman (Jordan). Amman's citadel marks the specific site of the ancient capital, which in the Iron II period was surrounded by a number of towers. Ammonite prosperity was derived from the trade routes they controlled.

David in his time reduced Ammon to a vassal state. As Amos notes (1:13), Ammon extended its borders northward in Gilead and held southern Gilead until the middle of the eighth century B.C.E. Gilead, the highland region east of the Jordan River, was occupied at times by its Ammonite neighbors to the south and its Aramean neighbors to the north. King Uzziah of Judah (783–742 B.C.E.) succeeded in gaining control of both Ammon and Edom. Under Tiglath-pileser III (745–727 B.C.E.) all Transjordan was reduced to Assyrian vassalage. In his turn, Sennacherib (704–681 B.C.E.) received tribute from Edom, Ammon, and Moab.

In the Iron Age II Ammonite remains (eighth to seventh century B.C.E.), there is evidence of destruction reminiscent of Amos 1:14, cited above. In present-day Amman, most of the visible archaeological material pertains to the Greek and Roman cities. In Hellenistic times (third century B.C.E.) Rabbah was renamed Philadelphia when it was captured by Ptolemy II Philadelphus.

Against Moab

> Thus says the LORD: "For three transgressions of Moab, and for four, I will not revoke the punishment; because he burned to lime the bones of the king of Edom. So I will send a fire upon Moab, and it shall devour the strongholds of Kerioth, and Moab shall die amid uproar, amid shouting and the sound of the trumpet; I

will cut off the ruler from its midst, and will slay all its princes with him," says the LORD. (Amos 2:1–3)

Moab is located east of the Dead Sea, in the center of Transjordan, with Ammon to the north and Edom to the south; Kerak and Dhiban (biblical Dibon) were its capital cities. Moab was protected in the Iron Age by a system of megalithic forts along the borders. The Moabites had frequent contacts with Israel and Judah. Both Saul and David achieved victory over Moab, Ammon, and Edom. According to 1 Kings 11:1, Solomon had among his hundreds of wives women from Ammon, Moab, and Edom, the result of political alliances, no doubt.

Much light has been shed on Moab and its relations with the Northern Kingdom of Israel in the ninth century B.C.E. by the discovery of the Moabite Stone (also called the Mesha Stele), an engraved stone celebrating a victory of Mesha, king of Moab (840–830 B.C.E.). When King Ahab of Israel died about 850 B.C.E., Mesha rebelled and succeeded in gaining independence from Israel. The king recounts his achievements on the black basalt stele, dedicated to Chemosh, national god of Moab, in gratitude for victory. This commemorative stele was found in 1868 at Dhiban, located on the King's Highway, east of the Dead Sea; it is now in the Louvre, the national museum of France.

Moab began to decline at the beginning of the eighth century B.C.E. Conquered by Assyria later in the eighth century B.C.E., Moab paid tribute to Assyria during the reign of Tiglath-pileser III (745–727 B.C.E.). Moab is often mentioned in Assyrian inscriptions.

Kerioth ("cities") has not been identified with certainty, although many sites have been proposed. Amos gives the impression it was strongly fortified. Kerioth is mentioned on the Moabite Stone as a main sanctuary of the god Chemosh.

Micah's Dirge (Micah 1:10–15)

The historical setting of this dirge was Sennacherib's military campaign in 701 B.C.E., when the Assyrian king conquered Lachish and several neighboring cities of the Shephelah (the low hills serving as a buffer between Philistia and Judah). Micah, a native of this region, was quite familiar with it. Not all the cities mentioned can be identified, partly because the Hebrew text is obscure and partly because Micah is punning on the names of the cities. Translations almost never convey such wordplays.

"Tell it not in Gath, weep not at all; in Beth-le-aphrah roll yourselves in the dust" (Micah 1:10).

Gath ("winepress") was one of the cities of the Philistine Pentapolis. It had been the home of Goliath in the days of the Judges. Amos omits it in his list of the Philistine cities (Amos 1:6–10), although he does mention "Gath of the Philistines" later (6:2). In his campaign against Ashdod in 712 B.C.E. the Assyrian Sargon II also destroyed Gath.

The ancient site of Gath has not been identified with certainty, but several proposals have been made. William F. Albright suggested Tell Sheikh Ahmed el-Areini (Tel Erani), situated fifteen miles east of Ashkelon, but it has been rejected because the Iron Age settlement on the site is too small for a city of Gath's prominence. More important, very little Philistine pottery was found there. Yohanan Aharoni and Anson Rainey have proposed Tell es-Safi (Tel Zafit), located twelve miles east of Ashdod. This was Frederick Bliss's suggestion when he excavated the mound in 1899. This site was occupied from about 3000 to 100 B.C.E.; there is ample evidence of occupation in Iron Age II (including the eighth century B.C.E.).

Beth-le-aphrah ("house of dust") may be identified with et-Taiyibeh, northwest of Hebron in the hill country of Judah, but this is not certain. Rolling in the dust (*'aphar*) is an expression of grief or mourning.

Shaphir, Zaanan, and Beth-ezel

> Pass on your way, inhabitants of Shaphir, in nakedness and shame; the inhabitants of Zaanan do not come forth; the wailing of Beth-ezel shall take away from you its standing place. (Micah 1:11)

Shaphir may be identified with Khirbet el-Qom, situated on a hill west of Hebron. William Dever conducted a salvage operation at this site in 1967, where he discovered Iron Age tombs with an inscription dating to the late eighth century B.C.E.. Khirbet el-Qom was first occupied in Early Bronze Age II; occupation ceased with the Babylonian destruction in the early sixth century B.C.E.

No information is available on Zaanan, but there is a wordplay of this name with the verb form "come forth" (*yaṣ'ah*).

Beth-ezel may be identified with modern Deir el-Asal, two miles east of Tell Beit Mirsim, which in turn is southwest of Hebron.

Maroth

> For the inhabitants of Maroth wait anxiously for good, because evil has come down from the LORD to the gate of Jerusalem. (Micah 1:12)

The ancient site of Maroth has not been identified. The wordplay consists in a contrast between the name Maroth, meaning "to be bitter," and the adjective "good."

Moresheth-gath and Achzib

Therefore you shall give parting gifts to Moresheth-gath; the houses of Achzib shall be a deceitful thing to the kings of Israel. (Micah 1:14)

Moresheth-gath ("possession of Gath") was the home of Micah; it has been identified with Tell Judeideh, situated about two miles north of Beit Jibrin (Eleutheropolis). Bliss and R. A. S. Macalister excavated this site in 1899 and 1900. First occupied in the Bronze Age (exact date uncertain), most of the remains date to the Roman period. Thirty-seven jar handles, stamped with the royal seal (*lamelekh*) and dating to the Iron II period, were also discovered.

Achzib is tentatively identified with Tell el-Beida, located northeast of Lachish. The pun in this verse is on the Hebrew root *kzb* ("to lie"): the name "Achzib" and "a deceitful thing" (*'akzab*).

Mareshah and Adullam

I will again bring a conqueror upon you, inhabitants of Mareshah; the glory of Israel shall come to Adullam. (Micah 1:15)

Mareshah, located at modern Tell Sandahannah (a corruption of the name of the Saint Anna Crusader Church), lies one mile southeast of Beit Jibrin (Eleutheropolis). Known in Greek as Marisa, this city became the capital of the Idumeans after the Babylonian exile. Bliss and Macalister excavated the site at the turn of the century. King Rehoboam of Judah (922–915 B.C.E.) fortified Mareshah, which defended the southwest approaches of Judah (2 Chron. 11:5–12).

The fortress city of Adullam may be identified with Tell esh-Sheikh Madkur in the Judean hills, five miles south of Beth-shemesh. David sought refuge from Saul in a cave near Adullam. Rehoboam fortified Adullam before the invasion of the Egyptians under Pharaoh Shishak of the Twenty-second Dynasty about 918 B.C.E.

3

Architecture, Fortifications, and Warfare

Grouping together architecture, fortifications, and warfare may at first seem arbitrary, but these topics are interrelated. The word "architecture" never appears in the Bible. Simply defined, architecture is the art of designing and building structures. It includes habitable installations of all kinds and the building materials utilized in their construction. The history of biblical architecture is complicated by the fact that only scanty remains are available to the archaeologist for reconstructing the buildings of antiquity. Several architectural features pertaining to defense, such as city walls, gates, fortresses, and towers, are treated in the section "Fortifications." The weapons of war, which are related to fortifications, are discussed in the section "Warfare."

Architecture ("House")

References to "house" in the Bible number some two thousand. "House" often designates a family dynasty; it may also refer to the dwelling of an ordinary person, of a king (palace), or of a god (temple).

Pillared House

The standard house in Palestine, from the eleventh century B.C.E. until the destruction of Judah in 586 B.C.E. was the pillared house, with variations of two, three, or four rooms. Yigal Shiloh has made a detailed study of the four-room house, which consisted of a broad room with three parallel oblong rooms extending from it. Many of the houses would have had two stories; the upper story was the living area and the lower was for food processing and storage. The partition walls consisted of stone pillars separating the middle room, a so-called court, from the other two parallel rooms. These side rooms appear to have been designed as domestic stables. The contiguous rooms were entered by doorways leading off the central room, where most of the domestic functions were performed. The pillars, in addition to serving as partitions, also supported the flat roof, or ceiling, if there was a second story. Whether one or two stories high, the entire structure very likely was roofed, although some think the central court was only partly covered. The walls of these buildings were constructed of stone foundations topped with mudbrick, and the floors were composed of stone and packed clay.

The simplicity of this architectural style made it easily adaptable for the construction of citadels and of monumental, administrative, and other public buildings as well as of private dwellings.

Shiloh believed the four-room house was exclusively Israelite in origin, but the fact that early examples have been found in Canaanite and Philistine contexts, as well as outside Palestine, points to a wider provenance. A four-room building of Late Bronze Age II (1400–1200 B.C.E.), found at Tel Batash (biblical Timnah) in the western part of south-central Palestine, makes it likely that these structures were of Canaanite, not Israelite, origin.

Excavations conducted in Palestine after World War II revealed remains of these typical pillared houses dating to the Divided Kingdom (922–586 B.C.E.). Roland de Vaux uncovered a four-room house from the eighth century B.C.E. at Tirzah (Tell el-Farah), the second capital in the time of the Northern Kingdom. Yigael Yadin made a comparable discovery at Hazor in Upper Galilee.

At Shechem, the first capital in the time of the Northern Kingdom under Jeroboam I, typical Israelite four-room houses were built on a series of terraces (Stratum VII [ca. 748–724 B.C.E.]). G. Ernest Wright, the excavator, described one of these houses (No. 1727) in detail. This house, almost exactly square (33 feet on each side), was constructed of stone and mud-plaster. In the second phase of construction, rooms had been added to the original building. It is of particular interest because the objects found in the central room (not an open-air court-yard, as Wright thought) provide insights into the daily life of the residents. They include a small storage bin, a large open hearth in the center, a large saddle-quern (a primitive hand mill for grinding grain), bottoms of clay jars set in pedestals of stone (to hold the ground flour or feed), and stone grinders.

Also discovered in connection with this house were an underground water system, querns, and silos. According to Wright, the ceiling construction consisted of beams of half logs, laid in pairs, with the rounded surface facing up and covered with a mixture of clay and straw mortar. Part, if not all, of this house had an upper story.

In the Jordan Valley at Tell es-Saidiyeh, tentatively identified as

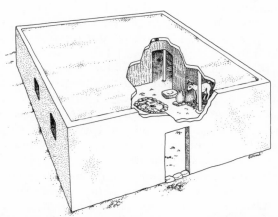

House 1727 at Shechem in the Northern Kingdom. This square pillared house, which dates to the eighth century B.C.E., was presumably destroyed by the Assyrian forces about 724 B.C.E. It consisted, *top,* of seven areas: numbers 1 and 2 indicate the central room with a large oval hearth (under the two-meter measuring stick); rooms 3 and 4 flank the court to the north, as do rooms 5 and 6 to the south; the long back room, designated as 7, was presumably the kitchen area, judging by the cooking fire and the storage bin.

It now appears that all the rooms of these pillared houses, including the so-called courtyard, were covered by a roof, as sketched, *below.* (The pillars would support either a roof or a second story.) Smoke from hearths and ovens would go out through the holes, which would have served also as windows. *(Courtesy of the Joint Expedition to Tell Balatah/Shechem; photo by Lee C. Ellenberger; drawing by Douglas Gilbert)* biblical Zarethan, where bronze utensils for the Temple were cast, excavator James Pritchard uncovered a housing development dating from the eighth century B.C.E. Of the ten almost identical houses, a typical one, consisting of a large room and courtyard, and a smaller room at the rear of the house, measured about 28 feet long and 16 feet wide on the inside. The roof that covered part of the large room was supported by four mudbrick columns.

Winter House and Summer House

In an oracle announcing the impending destruction of the luxury-loving people of the Northern Kingdom, Amos has the Lord state: "I will smite the winter house with the summer house" (Amos 3:15). This is a threat, but the exact meaning is ambiguous. Does the prophet envision two different parts of the same dwelling or two geographically separated dwellings? To achieve a measure of clarity, commentators invoke textual and archaeological parallels, which seem to favor two separate dwellings. According to the First Book of Kings, Ahab king of Israel had distinct palaces, one situated in the warmer climate of the Plain of Jezreel for winter (1 Kings 21:1) and the other on the hill of Samaria (v. 18) to catch the summer breeze.

The Book of Jeremiah refers to the "winter house" in Jerusalem of King Jehoiakim (609–598 B.C.E.): "It was the ninth month, and the king [Jehoiakim] was sitting in the winter house and there was a fire burning in the brazier before him" (Jer. 36:22). Unhappy with the oracles of Jeremiah, Jehoiakim contemptuously burned in the brazier the scroll containing the words of the prophet.

Using evidence outside the Bible, commentators invoke an inscription of Barrakab, Aramean king of Samal (in Turkey), roughly contemporary with Amos. He complains that until he built a new palace, the one built earlier by a predecessor, Kilamuwa, had to serve as both summer and winter palace. The inscription, found at Zincirli in 1891, reads: "My fathers, the kings of Samal, had no good house. They had the house of Kilamu [*sic*], which was their winter house and also their summer house. But I have built this house." This inscription was discovered near two adjoining palaces. The axis of one faced east to take advantage of the summer breeze; the other faced south to catch the sun and to serve as protection during the winter.

Ancient Samal, one of the Late Hittite city-states, is located in the foothills of the Anti-Taurus Mountains, in Turkey. Its modern site of Zincirli was excavated by the German Oriental Society from 1888 to 1892.

Ras Ibn Hani may also provide another useful parallel, since it may have been a summer residence at the shore for royalty living slightly inland at Ugarit (modern Ras Shamra). On a promontory on the Syrian coast, about three miles southwest of Ugarit, this Late Bronze Age site (1550–1200 B.C.E.), contemporary with Ugarit, has been excavated by Adnan Bounni. Of the large buildings uncovered there, one was especially imposing, with massive foundations. It may have been the summer palace constructed by the king of Ugarit.

These parallels, as well as the Hebrew wording of Amos 3:15, suggest that the prophet is referring to two geographically distinct buildings. Further, commentators wonder whether the passage in Amos 6:11: "For behold, the LORD commands, and the great house shall be smitten into fragments, and the little house into bits," relates to "the winter house with the summer house" of Amos 3:15. On the other hand, the "great house" may refer to the "houses of hewn stone" in Amos 5:11.

Houses of Hewn Stone

In denouncing the people of Samaria for exploiting the poor to satisfy their own greed, Amos warns, "You have built houses of hewn stone, but you shall not dwell in them" (Amos 5:11). Shiloh's special study of ashlar masonry is helpful in understanding this verse. Ashlar is dressed (hewn) stone which is squared into rectangular blocks with relatively flat sides. This dressed or trimmed stone is used in the construction of buildings and the laying of pavements. According to Shiloh:

> Two principal sorts of dressing can be distinguished on the surface of the ashlars: (1) A smooth dressing over the entire surface of the stone. (2) An irregular marginal dressing on one, two or three margins, with the face of the stone dressed leaving a boss [a rounded mass of stone] at the center.[1]

Dressed margins on the stones made it easier to fit these blocks into the walls with precision. The blocks were trimmed on the building site with a broad chisel and put in place one on top of the other entirely dry, without mortar. They were laid in alternating headers (with the short side toward the face of the wall) and stretchers (with the long side stretching along the face of the wall), as a way of strengthening the wall.

The finest examples of this building technique are at Samaria, where Omri and Ahab built the royal city in the ninth century B.C.E. Walls constructed of splendid ashlar masonry enclosed the royal quarter situated on the acropolis, the highest part of the city. This type of

Fine ashlar masonry at Samaria. The photo above illustrates the
"header-stretcher" pattern, in which the headers are placed over the
stretchers to enhance the stability of the wall. The segment of a long wall,
below, provides an example of stones with bosses and surrounding margins.
(Courtesy of the Israel Department of Antiquities and Museums)

construction contrasts sharply with the usual walls, consisting of stone foundations topped with bricks which were generally plastered.

Limestone quarries were near Samaria, and this fact accounts in part for the use of ashlar masonry there. The ashlars were cut out of the ground in the immediate vicinity of the hill where the city stood. The softness of the limestone made quarrying and dressing fairly easy.

Scholars trace the technique of ashlar masonry to the Phoenician culture. Aware that Hiram, king of Tyre, had sent skilled craftsmen to Israel at Solomon's request, they assume the same kind of export of skills a century later. In sum, ashlar masonry is very probably Phoenician, not Israelite, in origin.

Palaces

With an Assyrian attack imminent (perhaps 732 B.C.E.), Hosea announces divine judgment against the Northern Kingdom, which at the same time is an indictment of the people for their seeking false security in buildings instead of genuine security in God. He charges: "For Israel has forgotten his Maker, and built palaces *(hekal);* and Judah has multiplied fortified [Heb. verb root *bṣr*] cities; but I will send a fire upon his cities, and it shall devour his strongholds *('armon)''* (Hos. 8:14). *Hekal* generally means "temple" but is often translated "palace." In the same vein, Amos (5:9) and Hosea (10:14) both refer menacingly to the destruction of Israel's fortresses *(mibṣar,* from *bsr).*

'Armon, an architectural term, probably designates an especially fortified section of the royal palace. The word appears frequently in Amos' opening chapters, which are a series of judgments on foreign nations. Also, *'armon* is found four times in Amos 3:9–11, where the prophet indicts the people of Samaria for their arrogance, which, ironically, he invites the neighboring people to view for themselves.

Hosea may have had the famous palace of Samaria in mind as he proclaimed the oracles cited above. The royal palace, estimated to have measured 89 by 79 feet, was probably begun by Omri and completed by Ahab in the first half of the ninth century B.C.E. Later, during Amos' career, Jeroboam II reconstructed the palace. In addition to serving as the residence of the king, the palace functioned as the administrative center and as a law court. On the summit of the hill were located the royal quarters, enclosed by walls. Owing to the several destructions of Samaria as well as massive rebuilding, excavators have been able to define the palace only partially. Inferences about details of Israelite palaces can be gained only from parallels in other royal buildings in the Near East.

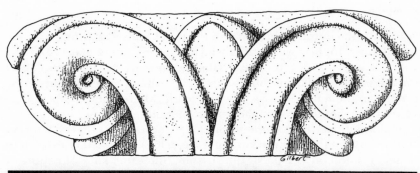

Iron Age II architectural ornamentation. The Proto-Aeolic stone capital from Hazor in the Northern Kingdom, *top,* which dates to the ninth century B.C.E., is one of the few architectural features that have been found in the major cities of Israel and Judah. Capitals of this style have been recovered from Jerusalem, Megiddo, and Samaria as well as from Hazor. The (restored) limestone balusters, *bottom,* dating to the late eighth to early seventh century B.C.E. were found in the royal Judahite palace at Ramat Rahel. They were used as railings for windows, as is evident from their appearance on the ivory plaque "Woman at the window" in chapter 6. (*Capital, courtesy of the Expedition to Hazor, Yigael Yadin, Director; drawing by Douglas Gilbert; balusters, courtesy of the Israel Department of Antiquities and Museums*)

Architectural Ornamentation

Two outstanding examples of architectural ornamentation in Iron Age II (1000–586 B.C.E.) are Proto-Aeolic capitals and balustrades; both have been found at Ramat Rahel and elsewhere. Midway between Jerusalem and Bethlehem is Ramat Rahel, identified as the site of biblical Beth-haccherem ("house of the vineyard"). The palace of the king (perhaps Jehoiakim [609–598 B.C.E.]) at Ramat Rahel is similar to the palace precinct of Samaria. It was adorned with Proto-Aeolic capitals, which are decorated with volutes (spiral-shaped ornaments) derived from the stylized palm-tree motif. These capitals have been found also in the royal cities of Jerusalem, Samaria, Hazor, and Megiddo.

The balustrade (a railing in a palace window) "consists of a row of identical colonnettes, each carved in the round in several sections, which include a flat-bottomed shaft, a wreath of drooping petals with molded rings of varying width above and below, and a voluted capital."[2]

The Jerusalem Temple

Temples and sanctuaries in general will be treated in chapter 4; only the Jerusalem Temple, owing to its importance in the economic and political life of Israel, will be considered here. Israel's builder par excellence was Solomon, known for his extensive building projects, notably the Temple of Jerusalem and the adjoining palace complex. The Temple required seven years to construct; the palace took thirteen years. Solomon's overly ambitious building program, in Jerusalem and elsewhere, caused serious social and economic problems, culminating in the secession of the Northern Kingdom of Israel.

The Jerusalem Temple was quite modest in size, measuring 90 feet long, 30 feet wide, and 45 feet high. No part of Solomon's Temple remains, so reconstruction is possible only by recourse to the biblical description (1 Kings 6–8; 2 Chronicles 2–4; also Ezek. 40:1–43:12) in the light of temples excavated elsewhere in the Near East, especially at Tell Tainat in the Amuq Valley at the northern Orontes (in Syria) where a small, long-room, tripartite temple was excavated in 1930. Built in the eighth century B.C.E., this temple bears close resemblance to Solomon's. Phoenician craftsmen, as well as Lebanese cedar and cypress, were provided by King Hiram of Tyre for building the Jerusalem Temple. It is not surprising that Solomon's Temple was modeled on Phoenician temples. Stone for the Temple was quarried near Jerusalem.

The Temple was a long-house building, rectangular in shape, with the entrance on one of the short walls. The interior of the Temple consisted of three sections, arranged longitudinally: the *'ulam,* or portico (30 feet wide and 15 feet deep), an unenclosed porch at the front of the Temple; the *hekal,* or main room (60 feet long, 30 feet wide, and 45 feet high); and the *debir,* or inner shrine, probably not a separate room, in the shape of a cube (30 feet in every direction). The Hebrew word *hekal,* borrowed indirectly by way of the Akkadian language, means "great house." The Temple itself is designated as *hekal,* or simply *bayit,* meaning "the house (of the Lord)." The *hekal,* or main room of the Temple, was also known as the "holy place" and the *debir* as the "holy of holies."

Two freestanding massive bronze pillars, about 40 feet high, were located at the entrance to the Temple, one on each side within the unenclosed portico. Perhaps symbolizing the "tree of life," these twin pillars were inscribed with curious names: Jachin ("he will establish") and Boaz ("in strength of"), possibly the opening words of royal inscriptions. The *hekal,* an elaborately decorated room, contained the sacred furniture, including the golden candlesticks, a small altar of cedar inlaid with gold leaf, and the table of the showbread (twelve loaves of consecrated, unleavened bread arranged in two rows). A double door crafted of pine led to the "holy of holies," which was lined with cedar. The Ark was placed within this innermost sanctuary, accessible only to the priests.

The palace complex, architecturally more imposing than the Temple, was composed of the House of the Forest of Lebanon, the Hall of Pillars, the Hall of the Throne, and the House of Pharaoh's Daughter. Archaeology can cast little light on Solomon's Temple and the adjoining palace complex, but the Bible is more helpful. Since the Six-Day War of 1967, Israeli archaeologists excavating in Jerusalem have illuminated many aspects of the city's history, if not directly the Temple of Solomon.

Fortifications

An invaluable modern study of biblical fortifications and warfare is *The Art of Warfare in Biblical Lands* by Yigael Yadin. As one of Israel's outstanding generals and leading archaeologists, he had excellent credentials for writing a book of this nature. Among the best ancient sources for fortifications and warfare in biblical times, especially in Iron Age II, in addition to the Bible, are the sculptures, wall paintings, and contemporary documents of the Assyrian kings, beginning with the war reliefs decorating the royal palaces of Ashurnasirpal II (884–860 B.C.E.) at Calah (modern Nimrud) and including those from the reigns of Shalmaneser III (859–825 B.C.E.), Tiglath-pileser III (745–727 B.C.E.), Sargon II (722–705 B.C.E.), Sennacherib (704–681 B.C.E.), and Ashurbanipal (668–627 B.C.E.). The discovery of the Assyrian sculptures, most of them dating from 900 to 600 B.C.E. when the Assyrian empire dominated the Near East, is an exciting story in itself.[3]

The classic example of Assyrian art with respect to fortifications and warfare is the series of detailed wall reliefs (pictures carved out of rock wall slabs) decorating a ceremonial room of Sennacherib's Southwest

Palace at Nineveh (modern Kuyunjik), uncovered in the middle of the nineteenth century (1846–1851 C.E.) by Austen Layard. Since he was excavating on behalf of the British Museum, many Assyrian sculptures are in London today. These graphic reliefs depict Sennacherib's storming and conquering, in 701 B.C.E., of the large Judahite garrison city of Lachish, second in importance to Jerusalem. An accompanying inscription identifies the beleaguered city as Lachish. These stone-carved reliefs, depicting the techniques of attacking and defending a walled city, have been described as the best extant example of military narrative art. They are an invaluable source of information for the excavators of biblical Lachish (Tell ed-Duweir), as the current director, David Ussishkin, readily acknowledges:

Assyrians storming Lachish. This famous relief is from Sennacherib's palace at Nineveh. Note the Assyrian soldier pouring water over the battering ram with a large ladle to protect its façade against the torches of the Judahites on the city wall. (*Courtesy of the Expedition to Lachish, David Ussishkin, Director; drawing by Judith Dekel*)

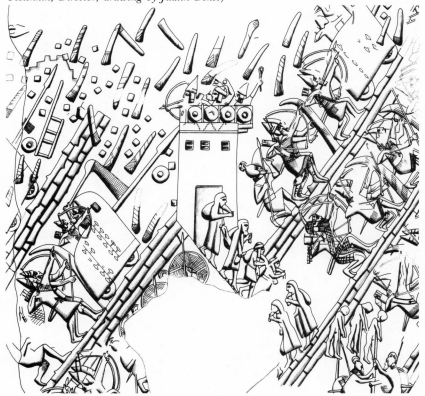

There is no other case in biblical archaeology in which a detailed Assyrian relief depicting a city under attack can be compared to the actual remains of that city and that battle uncovered by the archaeologist's spade, while the same events are corroborated by the Old Testament as well as the Assyrian sources.[4]

Palestine's vulnerable, albeit strategic, location at the crossroads of the ancient world, with Mesopotamia roughly to the northeast and Egypt to the southwest, required that the country be heavily fortified. In the Iron Age, during the United Kingdom (1000–922 B.C.E.) and the Divided Kingdom (922–586 B.C.E.) the cities were well fortified, but the method of defense was somewhat different during various periods.

City Walls

The basic fortification in antiquity was the wall, surrounding the city on all sides. Before 1200 B.C.E., these walls were thick and solid, generally consisting of rough-hewn stone foundations with mudbrick on top. In the Solomonic era (tenth century B.C.E.), the solid walls were replaced by casemates, which were already in use at several sites such as Taanach and Gezer in the Middle Bronze II period (1800–1650 B.C.E.). Casemates (strictly speaking, the casemates are the rectangular chambers, not the entire wall) consisted of two parallel walls, separated by five or six feet and joined at intervals by walls at right angles, creating a series of rectangular compartments. By filling the space between the outer (the thicker) and the inner wall with rubble, the casemates could be strengthened. At times, the chambers of the casemates, entered from inside the city, were utilized as residences or for storage. The casemates continued to be used in Judah until the destruction of the Southern Kingdom in 586 B.C.E. They were in use at Samaria in the time of King Ahab (869–850 B.C.E.).

By the end of Solomon's reign (922 B.C.E.), to combat the Assyrians' devastating battering ram, heavier and more massive walls had to be constructed. The new defenses took the form of offset-inset walls, whereby one section of the wall stuck out and the next section was set back. These angled projections allowed the defenders better control of the wall line. Dan, Hazor, Megiddo, and Beer-sheba are good examples of this kind of defense.

The city wall itself was protected and reinforced by several other installations, including glacis, fosses, and towers. A glacis is an artificial sloping ramp running downward from a wall on the outside to fortify it against enemy attack. Glacis-like structures were known already about 2500 B.C.E., but they were in common use in the Middle Bronze

Age (2000–1550 B.C.E.); by the ninth century B.C.E. the glacis had become highly developed. Many scholars maintain that the glacis was used to protect the base of city walls from the battering ram or as an antierosion device to hold the mound together. Lawrence Stager argues that the glacis was intended basically as a protection against sapping or undermining the walls of a city and sneaking in through such a tunnel.

The simplest form of the siege machine or battering ram, which originated with the Assyrians, was a long beam reinforced with a sharp metal head, equipped for bashing against vulnerable mudbrick walls. This beam or ram was suspended from the machine by thick ropes. The body of the battering ram, mobilized by four to six wheels, had a framework that protected its operators from the defenders' missiles hurled from the wall. The surface of the battering ram had to be watered down as protection against firebrands thrown from the walls. The Lachish reliefs vividly portray an Assyrian soldier pouring water from a large ladle over the ram.

Describing the imminent destruction of Samaria, to be followed by the deportation of its inhabitants, Amos addresses the women of Samaria: "And you shall go out through the breaches *(pereṣ)* [the gaps in the walls], every one straight before her" (Amos 4:3). In a contrasting salvation oracle in Amos, the Lord says, "In that day I will raise up the booth [the kingdom] of David that is fallen and repair its breaches *(pereṣ),* and raise up its ruins, and rebuild it as in the days of old" (Amos 9:11). The "breaches" to which the prophet refers were caused by the battering ram.

The fosse is a dry moat or ditch dug around the city wall as added protection against enemy attack. The wall of the city was further strengthened by towers built on each side of the gates or at other vulnerable points in the wall. In a salvation oracle concerning restored Jerusalem, Micah predicts: "And you, O tower of the flock (Migdal-eder), hill of the daughter of Zion, to you shall it come, the former dominion shall come, the kingdom of the daughter of Jerusalem" (Micah 4:8). Migdal-eder ("tower of the flock"), an ancient place name mentioned in Gen. 35:21, is here used symbolically of Jerusalem. In context, the reference is most probably to the fortified City of David.

In addition to the prophets' literal references to walls, they also use them figuratively. Addressing a prophecy of restoration to Jerusalem, Micah mentions "the building of your walls" as a metaphor for the reestablishment of the Jews in the promised land: "A day for the building of your walls *(gader)!* In that day the boundary shall be far extended" (Micah 7:11). The prophet most likely has in mind the walls of Jerusalem, though *gader* is not the common term for city walls. It usually signifies a fence of stones, of stones topped with plants, or a stone wall surrounding vineyards or fields, as in Isaiah's Song of the Lord's Vineyard (Isa. 5:5).

The walls of cities and houses are generally designated by Hebrew *ḥomah* and *qir;* in the context of fortifications, *ḥomah* appears to refer to the whole rampart, whereas *qir* is specifically used for the standing wall of the *ḥomah.* In his vision of the plummet, Amos reports: "He showed me: behold, the Lord was standing beside a wall *(ḥomah)* built with a plumb line, with a plumb line in his hand" (Amos 7:7). Further, in his oracles of judgment against foreign nations, Amos quotes the Lord as predicting in two cases: "So I will send a fire upon the wall *(ḥomah)* of Gaza" (Amos 1:7), and "So I will kindle a fire in the wall *(ḥomah)* of Rabbah [Amman]" (v. 14). Kindling a fire may refer to fire produced by wooden sleeper beams used in some ashlar walls—for example, at Megiddo. Or the reference may be to wooden ramparts or reinforcements which were part of mudbrick superstructures.

City Gate

The city gate, the weakest link in the fortification system, had to be flanked by towers and reinforced by such installations as bolts and bars of wood or metal to secure the gate. As a result, the gate complex was like a fortress. Besides fortifying the gate heavily, the military planners laid out the road to the gate in such a way that attackers would have to approach with their right side nearest to the wall. Since the shield was carried in the left hand, the attackers were exposed without protection to the missiles of the defenders.

A key text with respect to city fortifications, including the gates, is 1 Kings 9:15: "And this is the account of the forced labor which King Solomon levied to build the house of the LORD and his own house and the Millo and the wall *(ḥomah)* of Jerusalem and Hazor and Megiddo and Gezer." The Solomonic fortifications consisted of casemate walls, six-chamber gates, and twin towers. Archaeologists have verified that at Hazor, Megiddo, and Gezer there were three chambers and four piers on each side of the gate passage; whether the gate at Megiddo was connected to casemate walls is a moot point. A comparable four-entryway gate dating to the Iron II period has been unearthed at Ashdod; this gate remained in use until the Assyrians captured the city in 712 B.C.E. The gate at Lachish with its six chambers resembles the Solomonic gates at Hazor, Megiddo, and Gezer. It appears to have been built during the reign of Rehoboam of Judah (922–915 B.C.E.) and continued in use until Sennacherib destroyed Lachish in 701 B.C.E. The inner gate complex at Tel Dan (in the north) consists of two towers and four guardrooms. A bench at the right of the entrance of the main gate at Dan was also revealed. The excavator, Avraham Biran, attributes the building of this gate to Jeroboam I of Israel (922–901 B.C.E.). After 922 B.C.E., most gateways had only two rooms flanking each side of the gateways. From the early eighth century B.C.E. onward there were two-room gates, together with the four-chamber type.

The Solomonic gate at Gezer has been described as one of the most impressive remains from the period of the United Kingdom. Of ashlar construction, but not nearly so nice as the Megiddo ashlars, it had stone foundations, with a mudbrick superstructure. The three rooms on each side, opening onto the central passageway, were equipped with low stone benches. A large covered drain ran through the passageway of the gate.

The gate of an ancient city had wooden double doors, which were metal-plated to withstand fire. When the gates were closed, they were secured by a locking bar of bronze or iron which was positioned across the back of the double doors and held in place by sockets in the doorposts. In his judgment oracle against Damascus, Amos alludes to the bar securing the main gate of the city: "I will break the bar of Damascus" (Amos 1:5). Breaking the bars was a sign the city had fallen to the enemy.

The gate complex at Lachish (Area G), consisting of an outer and an inner gate, was larger than the Solomonic gates at Hazor, Megiddo, and Gezer. The inner gatehouse was a massive structure, measuring about 75 feet square, with four piers on each side. Its façade was flanked by two large towers. A stone-built channel through the passageway of the gate drained water from the roof of the gatehouse. The archaeologist Ussishkin mentions finding pieces of the bronze fittings of the gatehouse's wooden doors as well as lumps of carbonized wood attached to one of the bronze fragments, which he interprets as belonging to the wooden doors.

In addition to serving for defense, the city gate had several other functions. It was the place of assembly, and more important, it was the court where legal affairs were conducted. The benches along the walls of the rooms, contiguous to the gate, were for the city council elders who passed judgments and settled disputes. Owing to Amos' concern for social justice, he focuses sharply on the gate, synonymous with the court in his estimation, especially in his first "woe" speech with its three references to the "gate" (Amos 5:10, 12, 15). He describes the perversion of justice in these words: "They hate him who reproves in the gate, and they abhor him who speaks the truth" (v. 10). Contrary to the spirit of the law (Torah), which is aimed at protecting the righteous and helping the needy, exploitation and injustice were ram-

The Solomonic gate at Gezer. The best preserved of three Solomonic gates was uncovered at Gezer, eighteen miles northwest of Jerusalem. Typical of the Solomonic gateways are the three rectangular chambers on each side of the central passageway formed by four pairs of opposing piers. The gate had a stone foundation and a mudbrick superstructure. A drainage ditch ran through the central passageway.

In the photograph, people are sitting on the stone benches in the alcoves, where the elders would have conducted business, as Amos mentions. *(Courtesy of the Nelson Glueck School of Biblical Archaeology, Jerusalem)*

In the plan, *next page*, the entries are designated and the chambers are numbered. The installation in chamber 1 is a trough for watering animals. *(From* Biblical Archaeology Review 9 *[July/August 1983], 34–35)* pant in Amos' time: "For I know how many are your transgressions, and how great are your sins—you who afflict the righteous, who take a bribe, and turn aside the needy in the gate" (v. 12). Amos concludes his indictment of the people for their injustice at the "gate" with an exhortation to social justice: "Hate evil, and love good, and establish justice in the gate" (v. 15).

Micah also makes several references to the "gate." In a lament over Sennacherib's devastation of Judah, soon to include Jerusalem, he observes: "For her wound is incurable; and it has come to Judah, it has reached to the gate of my people, to Jerusalem" (Micah 1:9). In this verse the prophet considers Jerusalem as the center of the religious and civic life of the people of Judah. Continuing in the same vein, Micah says: "For the inhabitants of Maroth [a town in Judah] wait anxiously for good, because evil has come down from the LORD to [against] the gate of Jerusalem" (v. 12). Disaster is at the very gate of Jerusalem. In both of these passages of Micah, "gate" serves as metonymy for the city of Jerusalem itself.

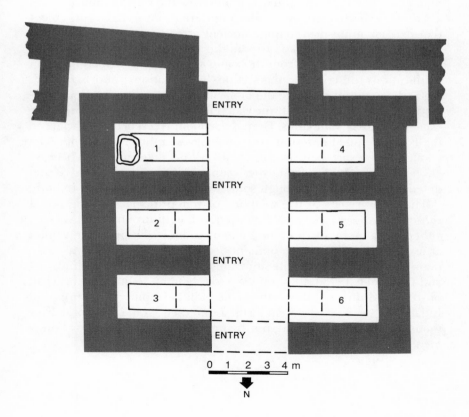

Micah 2:13 is a brief and hopeful interlude in the prophet's litany of social evils for which he charges the people of Judah. In a somewhat obscure verse, Micah or a later editor proclaims an oracle of salvation using the analogy of shepherd and flock, apparently to describe the restored remnant of all Israel: "He who opens the breach will go up before them; they will break through and pass the gate, going out by it. Their king will pass on before them, the LORD at their head" (Micah 2:13). The "gate" would symbolize the return from Babylonian exile after 538 B.C.E., not the release from Jerusalem at the time of Sennacherib's attack on the city in 701 B.C.E. Those who take the passage to be postexilic (after 538 B.C.E.) see it as a later addition to the Book of Micah.

Warfare

Warfare figures prominently in the Bible because it was practically a way of life in ancient times, although many of Israel's wars were defensive. The tendency today is to describe the wars of biblical times as cruel and barbarous, but modern warfare is not so different, except that it is far more devastating. Ancient armament was quite sophisticated, however. Information about the weapons and methods of warfare in antiquity comes from the same sources as information about fortifications (described in the section "Fortifications" above), including archaeological remains, the biblical text, contemporary documentary evidence, and especially the wall reliefs adorning the palaces of the war-minded Assyrian kings. Despite frequent references to warfare in the Bible, detailed descriptions of military weapons are lacking. As a result, their exact nature cannot always be determined. It is easy enough, however, to divide the weapons of war into offensive and defensive categories, although some weapons of war pertain to both.

The Bible refers to the weapons of war principally in the literal sense; nonetheless they are often used with figurative meanings. From a theological point of view, the Bible often looks disapprovingly upon arms and other military equipment because their use could easily diminish God's role as the sole source of security for the people of Israel and Judah. That God does not have to rely upon military means is an oft-repeated theme: "But I [the LORD] will have pity on the house of Judah, and I will deliver them by the LORD their God; I will not deliver them by bow, nor by sword, nor by war, nor by horses, nor by horsemen" (Hos. 1:7).

Offensive Weapons

Used both for hunting and fighting, the bow is one of the most ancient long-range weapons of war, dating at least to 3000 B.C.E. The components of the bow are the body, which is made of wood, and the string. In addition to the semicircular bow, there were the double-convex and composite bows. The latter, according to Yadin, were constructed of several strips of wood for resiliency, as well as sections of animal horn, animal tendons and sinews, and glue. This most powerful of the bows, with a range of three hundred to four hundred yards, is pictured clearly on the Assyrian monuments; it made archers the most formidable warriors of the infantry.

Assyrian archers. Two archers with composite bows take aim at the Judahites defending the city walls of Lachish. (*Courtesy of the Expedition to Lachish, David Ussishkin, Director; drawing by Douglas Gilbert from drawings of the Lachish reliefs by Judith Dekel*)

Arrows were tipped with heads made of flint, bone, or metal, of wood or reed bodies, and of feather tails. To free both hands for firing the bow, which was carried in the left hand, the archers kept the quivers on the back or over the shoulder. In combat the archers were protected by a full-length shield, often carried by a special shield bearer.

Describing an imminent military disaster, Amos quotes the Lord:

"He who handles the bow shall not stand [save his life], and he who is swift of foot shall not save himself, nor shall he who rides the horse save his life" (Amos 2:15). These figures of speech would have been clear to Amos' contemporaries, but as the variety of translations of this verse attest, the modern reader finds them somewhat ambiguous. In this verse Amos may be envisioning a two-man chariot, manned by archer and charioteer, not mounted cavalry. On the other hand, although the mounted cavalry dates only from the Persian period (538–332 B.C.E.) in Palestine, sometimes warriors did mount horses for a quick flight.

On the occasion of conferring the symbolic name Jezreel on the first child of Hosea and Gomer, the Lord spoke devastatingly: "And on that day, I will break the bow of Israel in the valley of Jezreel" (Hos. 1:5). "Jezreel" is reminiscent of the bloodshed wrought by Jehu when he destroyed the Omride dynasty (2 Kings 9–10). To "break the bow" is a symbol for destroying the military power of an enemy. When Tiglath-pileser III reduced Galilee in North Israel to vassalage in 733 B.C.E., this ominous prediction was fulfilled.

In contrast, once the people have been reconciled to God, the Lord will make the land safe by destroying the weapons of war, including the bow: "And I will abolish [break] the bow, the sword, and war from the land; and I will make you lie down in safety" (Hos. 2:18).

The sling, perhaps the most primitive of personal, long-range weapons, was used by both warriors and shepherds. It consisted of a hollow pocket of cloth or leather attached to two cords. The ammunition consisted of smooth, rounded stones, often flint, measuring two to three inches in diameter, carried in a bag suspended from the shoulder. With a stone placed in the pouch of the sling, the slinger would hold the ends of the cord and whirl the sling in the air to build momentum; then, releasing one cord, he would fire the missile with amazing accuracy.

In the Iron Age, slingers were a regular part of Near Eastern armies, as the Lachish reliefs at Nineveh attest. In depicting the Assyrian attack on Lachish, the reliefs show more archers than slingers. The Assyrian archers are positioned closer to the wall; the slingers were deployed farther from the wall, because it is impossible to sling a stone at a high angle.[5] Excavating the vulnerable gate area at Lachish, Ussishkin found far more arrowheads than slingstones.

"Sword" (Heb.: *ḥereb*), a metaphor for war and a symbol of oppression, is the most frequently mentioned weapon in the Bible. The one Hebrew word designates all types of swords, with no distinction in vocabulary between a sword and a dagger, which is a stabbing sword. Curved single-edged swords, sometimes called sickle swords, were

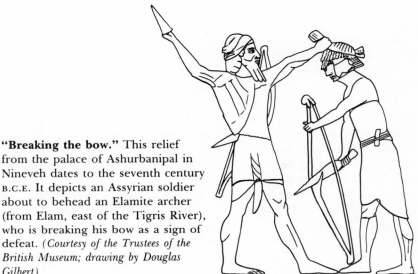

"Breaking the bow." This relief from the palace of Ashurbanipal in Nineveh dates to the seventh century B.C.E. It depicts an Assyrian soldier about to behead an Elamite archer (from Elam, east of the Tigris River), who is breaking his bow as a sign of defeat. *(Courtesy of the Trustees of the British Museum; drawing by Douglas Gilbert)*

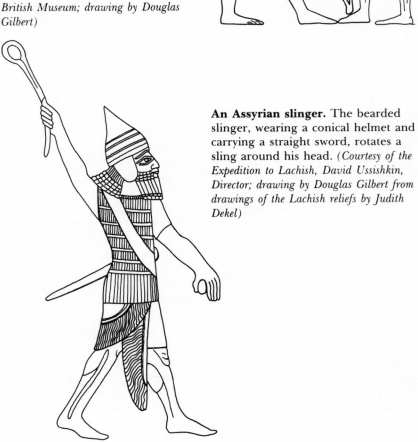

An Assyrian slinger. The bearded slinger, wearing a conical helmet and carrying a straight sword, rotates a sling around his head. *(Courtesy of the Expedition to Lachish, David Ussishkin, Director; drawing by Douglas Gilbert from drawings of the Lachish reliefs by Judith Dekel)*

used for striking or slashing; pointed double-edged swords, the more common of the two, were used for thrusting or stabbing. When iron replaced bronze in weapons (from the tenth century B.C.E. onward), the blades of swords and daggers became virtually unbreakable. The sword was the usual weapon for hand-to-hand combat.

In his judgment speech against Edom, Amos quotes the Lord: "For three transgressions of Edom, and for four, I will not revoke the punishment; because he pursued his brother with the sword, and cast off all pity, and his anger tore perpetually, and he kept his wrath for ever" (Amos 1:11). As today, rivalry and hostility were a way of life among the neighboring nations of the ancient Near East. The almost perpetual enmity between Edom and Israel can be traced back to David's era. Although Amos may be describing events in his own time or earlier, commentators are inclined to see in this verse a reference to events after the Babylonian conquest of Jerusalem in 586 B.C.E.

Predicting the impending destruction of the Northern Kingdom of Israel at the hands of the Assyrians, specifically Shalmaneser V (727–722 B.C.E.), the Lord says: "The sword [of Assyria] shall rage against their cities, consume the bars of their gates, and devour them in their fortresses" (Hos. 11:6). Aside from the reference to the "sword," the Hebrew text of this verse is uncertain.

In his classic statement on disarmament leading to universal peace, Micah predicts: "And they shall beat their swords into plowshares, and their spears (*ḥanit*) into pruning hooks" (Micah 4:3). As an economic measure, it was customary to convert discarded weapons of war into agricultural tools; ideally, war would be transformed into peace. This passage appears in substantially the same form in Isa. 2:4 (see chapter 5).

"Spear" (Heb.: *ḥanit*) is a generic term, including the javelin and the lance. An ancient weapon, the spear has a long wooden shaft, ending in a metal head; it was used for thrusting and stabbing. Bigger and heavier than the javelin, the spear was not thrown but was used with a forward movement. The javelin (Heb.: *kidon*), likened to a large arrow, was shorter than the spear and was used for throwing. The lance (Heb.: *romaḥ*), a spear with a long shaft, was a thrusting weapon. Some confusion arises when modern translators of the Bible use a variety of English terms to render the Hebrew words for weapons of war.

Among other offensive weapons were the ax and the mace. Hebrew has several words for ax, so it is difficult to be precise when the Bible does not give detailed descriptions of these weapons. An ancient instrument consisting of cutting edge and handle, the ax certainly was used for cutting and piercing in warfare; specifically, it was used against gates of cities. At the same time, the ax doubled as a tool. The mace, used for crushing, had a short handle, with a stone or metal head. Many other offensive weapons could be mentioned, but these suffice to give an idea of how the armies of ancient Israel were equipped.

Defensive Weapons

The shield, the helmet, and armor provided personal protection for the warriors. In hand-to-hand combat the shield was used in conjunction with the spear. Two Hebrew words for "shield" occur frequently, each designating a different kind of shield. *Magen* is a rather small, round-shaped buckler (usually worn on the left arm), as depicted in the Lachish bas-reliefs, whereas *ṣinnah* is a larger, oblong shield. The shield was held by a handle at the center on the inside. The ordinary shield was constructed of wood covered with leather, which had to be oiled for preservation. In addition to its literal meaning, in the Bible the shield is a metaphor for the protection provided by the king, and especially by God.

The helmet, part of the standard equipment, was especially useful for deflecting arrows fired at archers and charioteers. Originally of leather, the helmet was later made of metal. The typical Assyrian helmet was shaped like a rounded cone, with earlaps. On the Assyrian reliefs depicting the siege of Lachish, the Judahite warriors defending the city wear this Assyrian type of helmet.

Armor, a coat of mail of knee or ankle length for body protection in warfare, was especially useful for the archers and the charioteers, who were unable to carry shields to deflect missiles fired in their direction. It is assumed that the soldiers of Israel and Judah wore the same kind of armor as the Assyrian soldiers, as pictured on the bas-reliefs.

Chariots

The chariot, an important instrument of war, was introduced into Israel by Solomon to put his army on the same level as the neighboring peoples. This military innovation appears to have met opposition from his subjects, who considered the horse a sign of pagan luxury. Describing the succession to the throne of David, the author of the First Book of Kings writes: "Now Adonijah the son of Haggith exalted himself, saying, 'I will be king'; and he prepared for himself chariots and horsemen, and fifty men to run before him" (1 Kings 1:5). Absalom did the same when he forwarded his claim to the throne (2 Sam. 15:1). Commentators interpret these actions as signs of ambition and vanity.

Also, exclusive faith was to be invested in the Lord, not in instruments of war, as Isaiah declared: "Woe to those who go down to Egypt for help and rely on horses, who trust in chariots because they are many and in horsemen because they are very strong, but do not look to the Holy One of Israel or consult the LORD!" (Isa. 31:1).

The horse-drawn chariot as a weapon of war was known in Egypt from the time of the Asiatic invaders, called the Hyksos ("rulers of foreign hill countries"). Constituting the Fifteenth and the Sixteenth Dynasty of Egypt (1667–1559 B.C.E.), the Hyksos introduced the horse and chariot into Egypt. Operating well only on firm, level ground, the war chariot, built mostly of wood, was the Assyrian army's chief strength in open battle. Speed and maneuverability made the chariot especially effective in battle. Again, the Assyrian reliefs are an invaluable source of information about the war chariots of Iron Age II (1000–586 B.C.E.). It is assumed that the chariots of Israel and Judah had the same features as those of the Assyrians.

These wheeled vehicles underwent significant development in construction, but it is not easy to document. The body of the Assyrian chariot in the eighth century B.C.E. was the four-cornered box type, with the axle under the rear of the box. To make the chariots more stable and maneuverable, the four-spoked wheels were replaced by six-spoked wheels. By the ninth century B.C.E. the chariots were larger, with eight-spoked wheels. Each chariot had three horses, two in harness and one in reserve. As the chariots became heavier, the number of horses was increased to four. In the ninth century B.C.E. the Assyrian chariots were manned by a crew of two, a driver and an archer, who rode standing. In the time of Sargon II (722–705 B.C.E.), the crew almost always numbered three. On the reliefs, the third crewman, a shield bearer, is depicted holding two round shields; with one he protects the driver, with the other the archer. In the seventh century B.C.E. the crew was as large as four: driver, an archer, and two shield bearers.

Evidence about the war chariots of ancient Israel comes from the Bible, Assyrian bas-reliefs, stables discovered at such sites as Megiddo and Hazor (see chapter 6), and extrabiblical documents. According to the Annals of the Assyrian king Shalmaneser III, Ahab of Israel on the occasion of the battle of Qarqar (in Syria) in 853 B.C.E. supplied 2,000 chariots to help stop Assyrian aggression, whereas the king of Damascus, Ben-hadad I, was able to provide only 1,200.

The Israelites had no cavalry (soldiers mounted on horseback), nor did the Egyptians. The Assyrians, however, used cavalry in open battle, as attested on the palace walls of the Assyrian kings. To reduce personal vulnerability, cavalry archers in the reign of Ashurnasirpal II (884–860 B.C.E.) attacked in tandem: one fired the bow, while the other, at his side, held the shield and at the same time controlled the reins of both horses.

By the time of the prophet Jeremiah (626–587 B.C.E.), horse and chariot had become so common in Jerusalem that one of the city gates was named the Horse Gate (perhaps a chariot gate), situated at the southeastern corner of the Temple area (Jer. 31:40). Apparently, the people of Judah had overcome their opposition to the horse and chariot. As part of his reform, King Josiah of Judah (640–609 B.C.E.) removed from the entrance of the Temple the horses and chariots that his predecessors had dedicated to the sun (2 Kings 23:11).

Hosea rebukes the Northern Kingdom of Israel for placing false

An Assyrian chariot of the eighth century B.C.E. This basalt relief from the Hittite capital of Zincirli in modern Turkey depicts a bowman and a driver together in a chariot with six-spoked wheels. The bowman has a drawn bow in hand and a spear behind him; the driver has a whip in one hand and reins in the other. Under the horse is a prostrate enemy, naked and pierced with two arrows. (*Courtesy of the Museum of the Ancient Orient, Istanbul; drawing by Douglas Gilbert*)

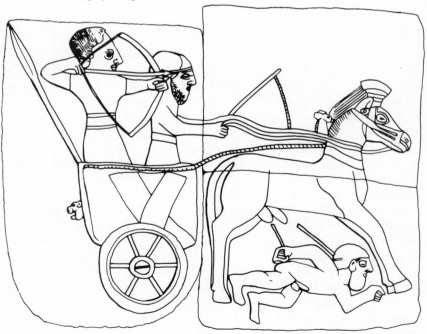

trust in military power, including chariots and warriors: "Because you
have trusted in your chariots and in the multitude of your warriors,
therefore the tumult of war shall arise among your people, and all your
fortresses shall be destroyed" (Hos. 10:13–14). Again, Hosea exhorts
Israel to return to God instead of seeking security in military might:
"Assyria shall not save us, we will not ride upon horses [war chariots]"
(Hos. 14:3).

Tauntingly, Micah reproaches the residents of Lachish for reliance
on horses and chariots, as Hosea and Isaiah did earlier. (Chariotry for
war is also forbidden in Deut. 17:16.) As the Assyrians were about to
advance upon the fortress city of Lachish, Micah states, literally: "Harness the chariots to the steeds *(larekesh)*, inhabitants of Lachish *(lakish);*
you were the beginning of sin to the daughter of Zion [Jerusalem], for
in you were found the transgressions of Israel" (Micah 1:13). There is
a wordplay in Hebrew on the city's name: *larekesh-lakish,* as is the case
with the other cities mentioned in Micah 1:10–15.

As part of the program of restoration for Jerusalem, Micah prophesies that the Lord will destroy Judah's military equipment, which has
been an unreliable substitute for God's providential care: " 'And in
that day,' says the LORD, 'I will cut off your horses from among you and
will destroy your chariots' " (Micah 5:10).

Siege Warfare

Siege warfare (sustained attack on walled cities), perfected by the
Assyrians, is well known from their bas-reliefs. It included several
techniques, among them circumvallation, the battering ram, and the
siege ramp. The simplest was circumvallation, signifying the complete
enclosure of a fortress so as to cut off the supply of food and water.
The battering ram, as already mentioned, was the war machine the
Assyrian besiegers used successfully against the defenses of Israel and
Judah in the Iron Age, despite the construction of the protective glacis.

Both the excavations at Lachish and the bas-reliefs at Nineveh confirm that the attacking Assyrians built in 701 B.C.E. a siege ramp outside the city wall at the southwestern corner of the mound, the most
vulnerable sector of the city because it was unprotected by deep valleys. Serving as a platform for the siege machines and the troops, the
siege ramp was wide at the base (180–198 feet) but narrower at the top
where it reached (52 feet high) the city wall. It was composed principally of cobbles and boulders piled on top of one another, with the
stones in the upper layer cemented together with mortar. Wooden
beams had to be inserted to stabilize the siege machines. According to
Israel Ephal, who has made a study of the military aspects of the

Assyrian siege ramp at Lachish, it would have required 1,000 porters about 23 days to build the siege ramp which was composed of 25,000 tons of soil.[6]

In response to the Assyrian attackers, the Judahite defenders of Lachish constructed a crescent-shaped counterramp inside the city wall, opposite the siege ramp of the Assyrians. The counterramp, extending about 360 feet along the inner city wall, was composed of thick layers of soil fill. This ramp served to strengthen the Lachish defenses and also acted as a platform from which the Judahites could return the fire of the Assyrians.

This unique discovery was made at Lachish in the 1983 dig season by director Ussishkin. As excavation continues there and elsewhere in Israel, Jordan, and Syria, archaeology will probably discover further evidence to illuminate warfare in biblical times.

4

Cult in Israel and Judah

This chapter deals with the religious institutions that are concerned with the worship of God. Worship and cult are basically the same, just as the worship of God and the service of God are synonymous terms. In earlier times it was thought that the deity had needs, and the deity's servants ministered to these needs. Primitive ideas about service to the deity underwent considerable development over the centuries. Several Hebrew words lie behind the concept of worship: the verb *hishtaḥavah* ("to bow down"); the verb *'abad* ("to serve") and the noun *'abodah* (translated "service"); and the verb *sheret* ("to minister," meaning to serve God in the cultic sense). Roland de Vaux defined cult as "all those acts by which communities or individuals give outward expression to their religious life, by which they seek and achieve contact with God."[1] These external forms which cult (*'abodah*) assumes are called ritual; cult cannot exist without ritual.

Passages such as the following from Amos led scholars of an earlier generation to judge that the prophets were anticultic:

> I [the LORD] hate, I despise your feasts, and I take no delight in your solemn assemblies. Even though you offer me your burnt offerings and cereal offerings, I will not accept them, and the peace offerings of your fatted beasts I will not look upon. Take away from me the noise of your songs; to the melody of your harps I will not listen. But let justice (*mishpaṭ*) roll down like waters, and righteousness (*ṣedaqah*) like an ever-flowing stream. (Amos 5:21–24)

"Justice" (*mishpaṭ*) and "righteousness" (*ṣedaqah*) are complementary, albeit complex, ideas in biblical religion, quite different from the Western understanding of the terms. No one Hebrew word can render the modern ethical concept of justice; it is included in the combination of *mishpaṭ* and *ṣedaqah*. Justice may be the right decision rendered by the judge "in the gate"; "righteousness," a term of relationship, means to be in right relationship with God. It denotes proper conduct for maintaining the demands of the covenant bond. In short, *sedaqah* is what conforms to the norm, namely, God.

Amos' severe judgment is a repudiation, not of the cult itself, but of the cult as it was practiced in the eighth century B.C.E. Cult was such an integral part of Israel's religion that the prophets could not reject the concept; the faith of Israel was expressed and preserved through the cult. It was as essential to Israel's faith as the Eucharist is to the Christian church.

The key to the proper understanding of the intention of Amos and the other prophets is found in the last verse of this quotation, referring to "justice" and "righteousness." To perform ritual worship without at the same time fulfilling the requirements of morality is meaningless. One's conduct in the marketplace must always conform to one's attitudes in the holy place.

Micah made the same point but more eloquently in his classic description of the Lord's controversy with those who had forgotten the covenant teaching that sacrifice is meaningless when unrelated to morality:

> "With what shall I [humanity] come before the Lord, and bow myself before God on high? Shall I come before him with burnt offerings, with calves a year old? Will the Lord be pleased with thousands of rams, with ten thousands of rivers of oil? Shall I give my first-born for my transgression, the fruit of my body for the sin of my soul?" He has showed you, O man, what is good; and what does the Lord require of you but to do justice (*mishpaṭ*), and to love kindness (*ḥesed*), and to walk humbly with your God? (Micah 6:6–8)

Ḥesed is one of the most profound concepts in the Hebrew Bible. Described as a gracious, loving deed, the word is really untranslatable. It implies a committed love on the basis of a previously established bond, a gratuitous love that goes beyond the call of duty. Love, mercy, and kindness are inadequate translations of *ḥesed;* it is no one of these virtues, but all of them together.

Hosea sounded the same notes as Amos and Micah concerning the moral requirements of Israelite religion: "For I [the Lord] desire steadfast love (*ḥesed*) and not sacrifice, the knowledge of God, rather than burnt offerings" (Hos. 6:6). "Steadfast love" and "knowledge of God," synonymous terms in Hosea's vocabulary, are possessed only in a personal relationship requiring complete commitment. "Knowledge" in this context is really "knowledge of the heart" which far exceeds intellectual apprehension, because it involves the whole person.

Basic to the teaching of the eighth-century prophets is the conviction that it is futile to profess love for God in the cult or any other form if one lacks love for neighbor. One is unlikely to love God if one does not love neighbor. Amos, Hosea, and Micah were convinced that love and righteousness are inseparable and that cult without them is meaningless.

While the opposition of the eighth-century prophets to cultic abuses is clear enough, the practices to which they objected are not so clear. Now, archaeology is contributing to the better understanding of cultic life and practice in the Iron Age (1200–586 B.C.E.). Recent excavations are yielding a number of significant cultic objects from the Israelite period as archaeologists investigate cultic sites, some of which the prophets mention by name.

Temples

Temple is an ambiguous word that can be used to denote a variety of places of worship. It usually identifies an architectural structure built for divine worship. On the basis of analogy, just as a person resides in a house, so too a god dwells in a temple. The building itself is designated as *bayit* (house) or *hekal* (palace), a term meaning "great house." The temple also functioned as an economic, cultural, and civic center. Unlike a church, the temple was not a place of public worship; the admission of worshipers was restricted to the courts of the temple. The word "temple" usually suggests the Temple in Jerusalem, but there were other temples as well.

Arad

On the eastern hill of Arad, one of Judah's royal border sanctuaries, Yohanan Aharoni discovered in 1963 the only Israelite temple unearthed in an archaeological excavation. This temple dedicated to the God of Israel was situated within a royal fortress which, along with the administrative center, was first built during the tenth century B.C.E. or later. The temple was rebuilt three times and may have been in existence throughout the life of the Iron Age fort. Contrary to Aharoni's opinion, there seems to be no basis for terminating the temple with the religious reform of Josiah.

The Arad temple is unlike the Jerusalem Temple; the temple of Arad is a broad-room type, with the entrance on the long side. The large sacrificial altar of earth and unhewn stones, in conformity with the directive of Ex. 20:25, stood in the courtyard. According to Aharoni, a flint slab covered the altar, equipped with plastered runlets for collecting blood of the sacrifice. The main hall or *hekal* was in the form of a broad-room. The "holy of holies," or *debir,* was located in the center of the wall opposite the entrance to the *hekal.* Three steps led upward to the "holy of holies," and its entrance was flanked by two small limestone incense altars, separating the "holy of holies" from the main hall. A well-finished standing stone or *maṣṣebah,* with evidence of red paint, was situated on a small platform within the "holy of holies."

Altars

The altar signified the presence of the deity; in the sacrificial ritual it was an instrument of mediation between God and the people. Unlike the Christian tradition, altars were generally found only in open air, that is, outside a building and independent of it. The Hebrew word for the altar is *mizbeaḥ,* derived from a verbal root meaning "to slaughter."

The sanctuary at Arad. This reconstructed sanctuary consists of three steps leading to a raised platform. On the top step are two stone incense altars flanking the entrance to the shrine and separating it from the broad-room at the bottom of the steps. At the back of the shrine is a stone stele *(maṣṣebah). (Courtesy of the Institute of Archaeology, Tel Aviv University; photo by Werner Braun)*

Originally the altar was associated with animal sacrifice; oblations in general were later included.

An altar took several forms; a large stone could serve the purpose, or even a pile of stones arranged in some kind of structure. The stones, however, had to be untrimmed in conformity with the covenant code: "If you make me an altar of stone, you shall not build it of hewn stones; for if you wield your tool upon it you profane it" (Ex. 20:25). Nor was the altar to have steps: "You shall not go up by steps to my altar, that your nakedness be not exposed on it" (Ex. 20:26). The altar could also be constructed of earth, or of metal, as in the case of Israel's central sanctuary.

Characteristic of the altar were projections or "horns" at each of the four corners; they may have been small *maṣṣebot* (sacred pillars). Their symbolism is uncertain, but the holiness of the altar bore a special relationship to the horns of the altar; the altar was consecrated by rubbing the blood of the victims on the horns. By grasping the horns of the altar, one gained asylum because the altar was sacred; this taboo was not always respected, however (1 Kings 2:28–35).

The Lord indicted Israel for multiplying altars: "Because Ephraim has multiplied altars for sinning, they have become to him altars for sinning" (Hos. 8:11). Instead of serving the laudable religious purpose of taking away sin, the proliferation of altars occasioned additional sin.

Amos' fifth vision took place at the altar: "I saw the LORD standing beside the altar" (Amos 9:1).

The burning of incense was an ancient ritual. Incense altars have been uncovered in large quantities at excavations in Israel, most recently at Tel Miqne (Ekron). These altars vary in size and shape; some are constructed of rectangular, hewn blocks of stone, with horns at the four corners.

High Places

High places (*bamot;* sing.: *bamah*) were open-air or roofed sanctuaries, usually located on high ground. These knolls or platforms were adorned with cult objects, including altars, stone pillars (*maṣṣebot;* sing.: *maṣṣebah*), and groves of trees (*'asherot;* sing.: *'asherah*). These religious places of worship, originally Canaanite, were an important part of the popular religion of Israel. Initially, they were not condemned, but the eighth-century prophets repudiated them because worship at the high places could easily deteriorate into syncretism (the combination of different forms of belief).

Hosea prophesied that God would punish Israel's idolatry by de-

Incense altars at Tel Miqne. A variety of altars dating to the seventh century B.C.E., including the four-horned incense altars, were uncovered at Tel Miqne (Ekron). *(Courtesy of the Joint Excavation Project, Trude Dothan and Seymour Gitin, Directors)*

stroying the places of cult and afterward convert them into a wilderness: "The high places *(bamot)* of Aven [Bethel], the sin of Israel, shall be destroyed. Thorn and thistle shall grow up on their altars" (Hos. 10:8).

In his vision of the plumb line, Amos heard the Lord saying, "The high places *(bamot)* of Isaac shall be made desolate, and the sanctuaries of Israel shall be laid waste, and I will rise against the house of Jeroboam with the sword" (Amos 7:9).

Pillars

Pillars, in Hebrew *maṣṣebot* (sing.: *maṣṣebah*), are standing stone monuments with a variety of functions, which Carl Graesser classifies under the following headings: memorial (as monuments honoring the dead), legal (as boundary markers or treaty stones), commemorative (as stelae marking a victory), and cultic (as signs of the divine presence).[2] The *maṣṣebot* may have been symbols of the male deity, just as the *'asherot* represented the female deity. According to Graesser, these standing stones could be plain or inscribed. The *maṣṣebot* in Egypt and Mesopotamia were inscribed, but not in Israel and Judah, unless the inscriptions had been painted on the covering stucco and the painted plaster no longer remains.

As part of the messianic restoration, idolatrous objects would be removed: "I will cut off your images *(pesilim)* and your pillars *(maṣṣebot)* from among you, and you shall bow down no more to the work of your hands [idols]" (Micah 5:13). In earlier times the *maṣṣebot* were considered to be legitimate; by the eighth century B.C.E. they were condemned.

Hosea 3 is brief but problematic. Describing his spouse Gomer's restoration as a sign of God's redemption of Israel, Hosea prophesies that the sacrificial cult would be terminated: "For the children of Israel shall dwell many days without king or prince, without sacrifice or pillar *(maṣṣebah)*, without ephod or teraphim" (Hos. 3:4). The identity of the ephod and the teraphim is not altogether certain; probably they were cultic objects used for divination. The ephod, however, is ordinarily understood as a priestly garment. The teraphim are usually thought of as figurines representing household gods, but some suggest that the term denotes cult masks worn by prophets associated with the temple, who spoke in the name of the deity.

Prophesying the impending destruction of Israel's religious institutions, Hosea stated, "Israel is a luxuriant vine that yields its fruit. The more his fruit increased the more altars he built; as his country improved he improved his pillars *(maṣṣebot)*. Their heart is false; now they must bear their guilt. The LORD will break down their altars, and destroy their pillars *(maṣṣebot)*" (Hos. 10:1–2). The more prosperous the Northern Kingdom, the more sinful its people. Prosperity led to destruction, because the affluent were more interested in themselves than in God and in others. The religious institutions of Israel became a vehicle for sinning under Canaanite influence.

Images

The second commandment (Ex. 20:4) of the Decalogue forbids the making of graven images; the fashioning of molten images is prohibited in Ex. 34:17. A graven image *(pesel)* is carved or sculptured from stone, metal, or wood. A molten image *(massekah)* is cast in a mold. Both kinds of representations of God were forbidden to the Israelites for a variety of reasons: God is spiritual; the image inevitably becomes identified with the deity; the transcendent God cannot be controlled, coerced, or exploited.

Hosea inveighed against Israel's attention to images in worship. The Lord indicted the Northern Kingdom for establishing under Jeroboam I a separate kingdom and independent sanctuaries with their own images: "They made kings, but not through me. They set up princes, but without my knowledge. With their silver and gold they made idols (*'aṣabbim* [from the root "to form"]) for their own destruction" (Hos. 8:4).

In a poignant description of God's parental love for Israel, Hosea indicted the "prodigal son" (Israel) for breaking the covenant by sacrificing to idols: "When Israel was a child, I loved him, and out of Egypt I called my son. The more I called them, the more they went from me; they kept sacrificing to the Baals [gods of Canaan], and burning incense to idols (*pesilim*)" (Hos. 11:1–2). This chapter contains one of the Old Testament's most sublime teachings about the unfailing nature of God's love.

Once again, the Northern Kingdom (Ephraim) was accused of idolatry. Ephraim had been highly respected until becoming involved with the fertility cult of Canaan: "When Ephraim spoke, men trembled; he was exalted in Israel; but he incurred guilt through Baal and died. And now they sin more and more, and make for themselves molten images (*massekah*), idols (*'asabbim*) skilfully made of their silver, all of them the work of craftsmen. Sacrifice to these, they say. Men kiss calves!" (Hos. 13:1–2). With respect to the "molten images," Hosea may have been thinking of Bethel, where Jeroboam I established a sanctuary and set up a calf image. As part of the ritual, the image of the deity was venerated with kisses, as Hosea noted, perhaps mockingly. Whether the calf image represents Yahweh or is only a pedestal for Yahweh does not appear to make a difference to Hosea.

In a divine judgment against Samaria, including a prediction of its destruction, Micah focuses on the worship of idols in the capital city: "All her images (*pesilim*) shall be beaten to pieces, . . . and all her idols (*'aṣabbim*) I will lay waste" (Micah 1:7).

Bulls

In the early 1980s a bronze figurine of a young bull was found on the summit of a range, near Dothan, in northern Samaria. It has been described as a finely executed piece of sculpture, seven inches long and five inches wide. On the basis of accompanying pottery, this bull has been dated to 1200 B.C.E. According to the excavator, Amihai Mazar, the figurine most likely was related to an open-air cult site, which he describes as an elliptical area about seventy feet in diameter, paved with flat stones and containing a large standing stone, possibly a *maṣṣebah*, as well as fragments of an incense burner and animal bones. Some scholars have concluded from the presence of these features that this enclosure had a cultic function in the early Israelite period, although this cannot be proved. It is not easy to distinguish between Canaanite and Israelite material culture of the Early Iron Age. If the site was cultic, one could not identify the specific cult on the basis of the fragmentary evidence.[3]

The bull was prominent in the Canaanite cultic tradition. A symbol of power and fertility, it was identified with the great Canaanite god Baal; it was a title of the god El as well as a symbol of Hadad, the West Semitic storm-god. In the Canaanite cult, the bull was the pedestal on which the image of the god was placed.

After the secession of the Northern Kingdom of Israel upon the death of Solomon in 922 B.C.E., Jeroboam I made two golden calves (sing.: *'egel*) which he placed in the sanctuaries at Dan and Bethel to discourage the Israelites from going to Jerusalem to worship in the Temple (1 Kings 12:26–33). Such visits could have resulted in the reunification of the divided kingdoms. Although the golden calves were intended to represent the throne of the invisible God of Israel, popular religion apparently identified them with the Lord.

A bronze figurine of a young bull. This Iron Age I figurine was found by chance in Samaria. The bull symbolized Hadad, the West Semitic storm-god, sometimes identified with Baal. *(Courtesy of the Israel Department of Antiquities; photo: Israel Museum, Jerusalem; Archaeological Staff Officer, Judea and Samaria)*

It was an easy matter to confuse the bull of Baal and the bull of the Lord; the bull throne signifying the presence of the God of Israel could easily become an object of worship. In the Iron Age the Israelites seemed always to be just a step removed from syncretism and idolatry.

The well-known incident of the "golden calf" in Exodus 32 describes how Aaron and the Israelites, in the absence of Moses, fashioned a molten calf which they then proceeded to worship. God repudiated them for this violation of covenant. This account, thought to be a later insertion into the Pentateuch, may be a subtle attack on Jeroboam I for setting up the bull cult in the Northern Kingdom of Israel.

The prominence of the "bull cult" in the Northern Kingdom is attested by Hosea's three references to it. In an indictment of Israel's national idolatry, he said, "I have [Hebrew "he has"] spurned your calf (*'egel*), O Samaria. My anger burns against them. How long will it be till they are pure in Israel? A workman made it; it is not God. The calf (*'egel*) of Samaria shall be broken to pieces" (Hos. 8:5–6). The royal city of Samaria had no bull image, so the reference must be to the idol erected in Bethel by Jeroboam I. This calf (or bull) seems to have been more than a pedestal for the Lord of Israel; it was worshiped as an idol.

Describing the apprehension of the Israelites about the security of their idol, Hosea observed, "The inhabitants of Samaria tremble for the calf (*'egel*) of Beth-aven [Bethel]. Its people shall mourn for it, and its idolatrous priests shall wail over it, over its glory which has departed from it" (Hos. 10:5).

"Beth-aven" (literally, "house of iniquity" or "house of nothingness") is, as already noted, a contemptuous term for Bethel ("house of God"). ("Beth-aven" also appears in Hos. 4:15 and 5:8.) This disparaging nickname for Bethel can be traced to Amos, who punned, "Bethel shall come to nought (*'aven*)" (Amos 5:5).

As a further consideration, the priests of Baal wore masks bearing the image of a bull when performing their ritual worship. A Syrian representation of Baal himself portrays the god in human form, with the horns of a bull on his forehead.

Asherah

Whether a goddess was worshiped in ancient Israel is a matter of dispute, but the eighth-century prophets uttered powerful polemics against female deities. The Old Testament contains some forty references to Asherah, denoting a cultic practice adapted from Israel's neighbors. It is sometimes difficult to distinguish the precise meaning

"Baal of the lightning." This white limestone stele of uncertain date (perhaps fourteenth to thirteenth century B.C.E.) was found in a sanctuary at Ugarit (Ras Shamra) in Syria. Baal is represented brandishing a thunderbolt. The lance in the god's left hand is decorated with branches that may symbolize lightning. On his helmet are the horns of a bull.
(Courtesy of the Louvre National Museum of France, Paris; drawing by Douglas Gilbert)

of Asherah in the Hebrew Bible; it may be a goddess personified or a cultic object.

In Canaanite religion Asherah was a mother goddess, with emphasis on breasts, lactation, procreation, and fertility. She was a fertility goddess, a consort of the god El in the texts from Ugarit (Ras Shamra), known for its religious and mythological texts which are closely related to the Hebrew Bible. The cult of Asherah was popular in both Israel and Judah, where the goddess was considered a consort of the god Baal. Asherah was distinct from two other Canaanite goddesses of fertility, Astarte and Anath. Astarte, the Greek form of the Hebrew name Ashtoreth, was also a female consort of the Canaanite god El. In Ugaritic literature, Anath, the sister and consort of Baal, was the goddess of war.

As a cultic object, Asherah very likely had the form of a wooden pole, which symbolized the goddess. Other conjectures have been made about the shape of this object, including a sacred tree placed beside the altar in a sanctuary, or a wooden object, which was carved from a tree trunk and stood upright. That it was wooden seems clear from the several Hebrew verbs used in connection with Asherah in the Bible: "You shall . . . cut down *(karat)* their Asherim" (Ex. 34:13); "You shall

... hew down (*gida'*) their Asherim" (Deut. 7:5); "You shall . . . burn (*sarap*) their Asherim with fire" (Deut. 12:3).

Closely related to the Canaanite goddesses of fertility are small, nude fertility figurines of clay found frequently in private residences in Israel and Judah, even in Jerusalem. Dating to the Iron Age (1200–586 B.C.E.), they may represent Asherah or Astarte; they were used apparently as amulets to ensure fertility. They are called "fertility figurines" because of the exaggerated size of the sexual organs, especially the breasts, which are supported by the hands. The eighth-century prophets denounced all such cultic objects because the people ran the risk of deifying them and consequently making them rivals of Israel's God. Canaanite and Israelite practices were so intertwined that the people of Israel were frequently but one step removed from syncretism.

Like the fertility figurines, cult prostitution was a popular aspect of the Canaanite fertility cult. This practice too was adopted from Canaan

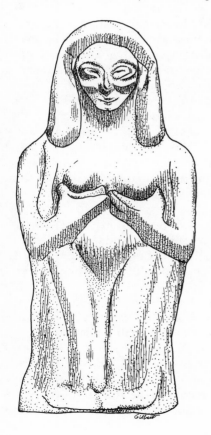

A Phoenician Ashtoreth clay figurine. Dating from the seventh to the sixth century B.C.E., this pregnant Ashtoreth was found at Tel Dor (in Israel) in 1985. (*Courtesy of the Expedition to Tel Dor, Ephraim Stern, Director; drawing by Douglas Gilbert*)

by the Israelites, much to the chagrin of the prophets. The religious prostitute, designated in Hebrew as *qedeshah* ("holy woman"), represented the goddess of fertility. Scholars dispute whether Gomer, spouse of Hosea, was a temple prostitute or a faithless wife.

By way of background, in the view of the Canaanites religion and agriculture were interrelated, with the cycles of nature dependent upon sexual relations between the gods, especially Baal and his female partner Astarte. Sexual intercourse of the deities was responsible for the fertility of the land and the resultant harvest. To assist the process, male and female prostitutes who were associated with the temple engaged in illicit sexual relations with visitors to the temple. Imitating divine actions in this manner in order to affect fertility of the soil was a form of sympathetic magic.

A common motif pertaining to sacred prostitution is the "woman at the window," known from several sites in the Near East. In the guise of a sacred prostitute wearing an Egyptian type of wig, she gazes from her window, overlooking a balcony balustrade; she has an alluring smile to attract prospective passers-by. In his exhortation to repentance, Jeremiah depicted Israel as a faithless spouse, saying, "You have a harlot's brow, you refuse to be ashamed" (Jer. 3:3). Some commentators detect in Jeremiah a reference to the frontlet or phylactery adorning the "woman at the window." The "woman at the window" may represent the Phoenician goddess Ashtart or a related goddess; as a sacred prostitute she peeps through the window at her lover.

The following texts from the eighth-century prophets condemn one or another aspect of the Asherah cult. Micah prophesied that as part of the messianic restoration the Lord would purge the land of pagan cult objects. He mentioned explicitly the Asherim (plural form): "I [the LORD] will root out your Asherim from among you and destroy your cities" (Micah 5:14).

In his indictment of the cult, Hosea, quoting the Lord, listed among the abuses: "My people inquire of a thing of wood, and their staff gives them oracles" (Hos. 4:12). Although Asherah is not mentioned specifically, the divination described could be affected through a tree or pole erected next to the altar.

Alluding to the idolatrous worship offered from Dan to Beer-sheba, the northern and southern extremities of the Northern Kingdom, Amos mentions that "those who swear by Ashimah (*'ashmath*) of Samaria, and say, 'As thy god lives, O Dan,' and, 'As the way of Beer-sheba lives,' they shall fall, and never rise again" (Amos 8:14). The Hebrew *'ashmath* is variously interpreted, as modern translations attest. If "Ashimah" is correct, the reference is to the goddess of Hamath (the modern city of Hama in Syria), whose cult was introduced into

Samaria after the fall of the Northern Kingdom in 721 B.C.E. If one reads *'ashmah,* meaning "guilt," "the guilt of Samaria" may refer to the royal sanctuary at Bethel. Some suggest amending the text to read "Asherah," but there is no need to substitute Asherah for Ashimah, because the deity does seem to exist.

Among the transgressions of Israel, Amos lists, "A man and his father go in to the same maiden *(na'arah),* so that my holy name is profaned" (Amos 2:7). Although Amos does not use the technical Hebrew term, *qedeshah,* for a cult prostitute, the context lends credence to such an interpretation.

Unquestionably, Hosea had ritual prostitution in mind in his indictment of Israel's cult: "I will not punish your daughters when they play the harlot, nor your brides when they commit adultery; for the men themselves go aside with harlots, and sacrifice with cult prostitutes *(qedeshot),* and a people without understanding shall come to ruin" (Hos. 4:14).

Temple prostitution was more reprehensible than harlotry which was common in Israel. Sacred prostitution was explicitly repudiated: "There shall be no cult prostitute *(qedeshah)* of the daughters of Israel, neither shall there be a cult prostitute *(qadesh)* of the sons of Israel" (Deut. 23:17).

Cultic Buildings

The cultic buildings located in the royal cities of both Israel and Judah during the Iron II period were frequently the object of prophetic attack. In addition to Dan in the Northern Kingdom, cities such as Beer-sheba and Jerusalem in the Southern Kingdom were denounced.

Dan

Recent excavations at Dan have revealed the sacred area, or temenos, measuring over a half acre. Part of this sacred area may be a high place, or *bamah,* according to excavator Avraham Biran, who suggests that it was erected by Jeroboam I and later enlarged by Ahab; it dates from the tenth century B.C.E. and continued in use to the eighth century B.C.E. If the *bamah* is part of the sanctuary built by Jeroboam I, no trace of the golden calf has come to light. The cultic installation tentatively identified as a high place was thought to be an open-air sanctuary. It has been described as a large square podium, about 54 × 54 feet, enclosed by walls and filled with basalt and fieldstones.

More recent excavations have confirmed that to the west of the high place there was a temple atop the great platform at Dan. An altar and

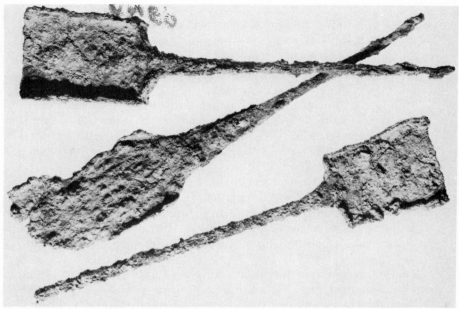

Incense shovels from Dan. Three iron incense shovels, each about 20 inches long, were uncovered at Dan, west of the high place *(bamah)*. Mentioned in the Bible as *maḥtah* and *ya'eh,* these shovels are known from Roman and Byzantine synagogues. *(Courtesy of the Nelson Glueck School of Biblical Archaeology, Jerusalem)*

three iron incense shovels, as well as a jar of ashes, have been uncovered. Biran dates this sanctuary about 800 B.C.E.

Beer-sheba

In the 1973 excavation season at Tel Beer-sheba, Aharoni discovered almost half the stones of a large horned altar. These were found in a restored section of a storehouse wall, dating from the eighth century B.C.E. Three of the four horns of the altar were found intact; the top of the fourth had been knocked off. Contrary to the biblical law requiring that altars be built of unhewn stones (Ex. 20:25), the stones of this altar were ashlar masonry. After reconstructing the altar, Aharoni concluded that its original height was just over five feet. He also conjectured that this horned altar had been dismantled and then reused in the wall at the time of the religious reform of Hezekiah (715–687 B.C.E.), which required that worship be centralized in Jerusalem.

A snake, the symbol of fertility, was engraved on one of the altar stones. It may have been reminiscent of the bronze serpent from the Mosaic era which later was venerated in the Jerusalem Temple. During the serpent scourge in the wilderness, Israelites bitten by venomous serpents were healed when Moses lifted up a bronze serpent (Num. 21:4–9).

In an oracle of doom against Bethel, one of the principal royal sanctuaries of the Northern Kingdom, Amos quoted the Lord: "I will punish the altars of Bethel, and the horns of the altar shall be cut off and fall to the ground" (Amos 3:14). The cultic tradition concerning Bethel went back to the patriarch Jacob, who set up a sacred stone (*maṣṣebah*) there to commemorate his vision of the "ladder" (Gen.

A horned altar at Beer-sheba. The stones of this five-foot-high reconstructed limestone altar were found incorporated into storehouse walls at Beer-sheba. (*Courtesy of the Institute of Archaeology, Tel Aviv University; photo by Avraham Hay*)

28:10–22). To break off the horns or projections at the four corners of the altar was to desecrate it.

According to Amos, the Israelites made religious pilgrimages to the Southern Kingdom of Judah, including the sanctuary at Beer-sheba. The Lord had rejected all these sanctuaries, however: "Do not seek Bethel, and do not enter into Gilgal or cross over to Beer-sheba; for Gilgal shall surely go into exile, and Bethel shall come to nought" (Amos 5:5).

Kuntillet Ajrud

In 1975 and 1976, Zeev Meshel excavated a remote wayside shrine in northeastern Sinai which is casting light on Asherah, understood either as a cultic object or as the goddess of Iron Age II (1000–586 B.C.E.). The remains uncovered there reflect the practices of popular religion in the eighth century B.C.E. and seem to justify the severe condemnation of the prophets.

The site, located about forty miles south of the large oasis of Kadesh-barnea, is known in Arabic as Kuntillet Ajrud, meaning "the solitary hill of the water wells," which is an accurate topographical description; in Hebrew it is called Horvat (ruin of) Teiman. This religious center, which was the southernmost outpost of the Judahite kingdom, included a main building (West Building) as well as a smaller one, but little remains of it.

The most remarkable discoveries at Kuntillet Ajrud are the inscriptions and the drawings. Hebrew and Phoenician inscriptions decorated the plaster walls of the building, two large storage jars (*pithoi*), and stone vessels. Crude drawings appear on the walls and the storage jars, although the connection, if any, between the drawings and the inscriptions is still uncertain.

On the basis of the pottery and the inscriptions, Meshel dates the site about 800 B.C.E., when Amaziah (800–783 B.C.E.) was king of Judah and Joash (801–786 B.C.E.), the father of Jeroboam II, was king of Israel. Having achieved victory over Aram and Judah, reducing Judah practically to vassalage, Joash prepared the way for Jeroboam II, one of the greatest kings of Israel.

One of the inscriptions reads, "I bless you by Yahweh of Samaria and by his asherah." The reference to Samaria indicates the influence of the Northern Kingdom on Kuntillet Ajrud. It is unlikely that "his asherah" is a reference to the goddess, because biblical Hebrew does not use personal names with a pronominal suffix. If the grammatical argument is decisive, then "asherah" may signify a cultic object, the wooden symbol of the goddess, or a sacred tree or grove.

At Khirbet el-Qom, eight miles west of Hebron, William Dever excavated some Iron Age tombs in the late 1960s. On the wall of a tomb was a funerary inscription with a reference to asherah: "Blessed by Yahweh and by his asherah."

The drawings on the storage jars at Kuntillet Ajrud are more puzzling than the inscriptions. Under the inscription just discussed are depicted two standing figures and a seated woman playing a lyre *(kinnor)*. Scholarly opinion varies about the identity of the figures. The two standing figures, according to art historian Pirhiya Beck, represent the god Bes, a designation for the Egyptian dwarf deities. Beck calls attention to the grotesque faces of these figures as well as their feathered

The jar drawings at Kuntillet Ajrud. Scholars identify these figures diversely. Pirhiya Beck, who has done the most complete study, identifies both standing figures as representations of the god Bes but says the lyre player is not a goddess. (*"The Drawings from Horvat Teiman [Kuntillet Ajrud],"* Tel Aviv 9 *[1982]:3–68; courtesy of the Expedition to Kuntillet Ajrud, Zeev Meshel, Director; drawings by H. Kek and N. Schechter, Studies of the Institute of Archaeology, Tel Aviv University*)

headdress, nudity, and the akimbo position of their arms. While maintaining that the lyre player is not a goddess, Beck points out that Bes is often associated with music and dancing. She also calls attention to the Phoenician style of these drawings.

Positing a connection between the inscription and the drawing on the storage jar, Michael Coogan suggests that the standing figures do not represent Bes; rather, the figure to the left is Yahweh and the one on the right is his consort Asherah. Persuaded by the prophets' (especially Hosea's) "use of the marriage metaphor to describe the relationship between Yahweh and Israel," Coogan makes this assertion: "The ubiquitous female figurines from Iron Age sites throughout the Levant seem even more likely than earlier thought to be representations of the divine consorts of the respective national deities."[4]

On the basis of the inscriptions and the drawings, as well as the presence of Samaria ware and Phoenician-style pottery, there appears to be an influence of the Northern Kingdom and Phoenicia upon the wayside shrine of Kuntillet Ajrud. Additional evidence may come from the fact that Athaliah had Phoenician lineage; the daughter of Ahab and Jezebel, she reigned over Judah from 842 to 837 B.C.E., after the death of her son Ahaziah, who ruled but one year.

Taanach

Located five miles southeast of Megiddo in the Northern Kingdom of Israel, Taanach was an important city first settled in the Early Bronze Age (3300–2000 B.C.E.). It is well known for the battle in which Deborah and Barak defeated the Canaanites about 1125 B.C.E., memoralized in the Song of Deborah (Judges 5).

A unique and elaborate cultic stand of the tenth century B.C.E.,

Canaanite cultic stand at Taanach. The Taanach cultic stand dating to the tenth century B.C.E. measures twenty-one inches high. Square and hollow, this stand has four elaborately decorated registers, including the goddess with lions on the bottom register and the prominent bull calf on the top, perhaps symbolizing Baal-Hadad. (*Courtesy of the Israel Department of Antiquities; photo: Israel Museum, Jerusalem; Archaeological Staff Officer, Judea and Samaria*)

found at Taanach during Paul Lapp's excavations in the 1960s, is casting important light on Iron Age cult. Less than two feet high and of poorly fired clay, this cultic stand is constructed of "four superimposed hollow squares topped by a ridged basin." Lapp speculated that the stand was used for libations or offerings, because there was no evidence of burning or incense.

The stand is decorated with a variety of images traditionally associated with the cult. On the lowest register is a naked female figure, described as "Astarte type," facing front and flanked by two lions. This may be a personification of the mother goddess Asherah. On the next register are a pair of winged sphinxes with lions' bodies and female heads. The third register depicts goats or ibexes nibbling from a stylized tree and flanked by two lions. This sacred tree may also represent Asherah. It is significant that at Kuntillet Ajrud one of the storage jars is decorated with a sacred tree flanked by two ibexes, along with a lion, in conjunction with the inscription mentioning Asherah. The top register exhibits prominently a bull calf (without horns) surmounted by a winged sun disk, which may represent the deity Baal-Hadad, who is associated with the bull. Interpreting the naked female figure on the lowest register as the goddess Asherah, David Noel Freedman is inclined to identify the bull calf on the top register as Yahweh.[5]

The identification and significance of the rich imagery adorning the cultic stand at Taanach are still under discussion. A recent article by Ruth Hestrin of the Israel Museum has appeared, and it should help to clarify the nature and function of this stand. Hestrin identifies the young bull on the top register as Baal, and she identifies the naked woman on the bottom register, as well as the tree of the third register, as Asherah. In her estimation the Taanach cultic stand was intended for the worship of Baal and Asherah.[6]

Like many other aspects of the eighth century B.C.E. the cult is occupying the attention of scholars today. It is hoped that their research may help to illuminate several of the issues raised in this chapter.

5

Agriculture, Plants, and Animals

Michael Zohary, late professor of botany at the Hebrew University in Jerusalem, wrote extensively on the plants of Palestine. Describing agriculture in the Bible, he stated:

> Scarcely does any other ancient book offer so rich and vivid a picture of agricultural life as the Bible. . . . The social structure, livelihood, and domestic life of the ancient Israelite family revolved almost exclusively around agriculture, whose various activities are frequently mentioned in biblical parables.[1]

Ecology, including agriculture, plants, and animals, is not only the language of nature but also the setting of the Bible.

Agriculture

In biblical times agriculture was an important occupation impinging on almost every aspect of life, including religion. It was the basis of the economy, because the majority of the population were farmers. For the Iron Age, when fruit trees and grains were the principal crops, the Bible is a primary source of information about agriculture. Biblical literature, especially the eighth-century prophets, is full of metaphors drawn from the agricultural life of people who were close to the soil.

A farmer in Palestine has never had an easy life; the land is stony and hilly, the sirocco (a hot, dust-laden wind) is oppressive, and the insects and blight are devastating. Despite these obstacles, the farmers of biblical times managed to survive, as do their counterparts today.

The sources of water, in addition to rainfall, were cisterns, springs, wells, tributary streams, and especially dew. Farming was done mainly without artificial irrigation. In the Iron Age the terracing of hills made them suitable for dry farming (nonirrigated farming by moisture-conserving plowing and with drought-resistant plants). Desert farming was also done in the Iron Age. Usually olive trees and vines were planted on the slopes, and cereals were sown in the valleys. As Hosea confirms, "the grain, the wine, and the oil" (Hos. 2:8) were the three dominant agricultural products in ancient Israel.

To describe the glorious age to come as a time of peace, prosperity, and plenty, Amos borrows several metaphors from agricultural life. His text is both optimistic and vivid: " 'Behold, the days are coming,' says the LORD, 'when the plowman shall overtake the reaper and the treader of grapes him who sows the seed; the mountains shall drip sweet wine, and all the hills shall flow with it. I will restore the fortunes of my people Israel, and they shall rebuild the ruined cities and inhabit them; they shall plant vineyards and drink their wine, and they shall make gardens and eat their fruit' " (Amos 9:13–14).

In the age to come the fertile land would be so productive that the agricultural cycles, without the natural intermissions, would seem to overlap. The barley and wheat would no sooner be harvested than it would be time for plowing; the pressing of grapes would not be completed before the sowing began. Such abundance of grain and wine, as described by Amos, symbolizes the fullness of life.

According to the usual agricultural cycle in Palestine, plowing was undertaken only after the first rainfall in October or November had loosened the soil; then the sowing of seed followed. Barley and wheat were planted at the same time, in late October or early November. The wheat was harvested in May or June, the barley a month earlier. The grapes were gathered for vintage in August and September.

The people of ancient Israel celebrated three major pilgrimage festivals: Passover (Heb.: *pesaḥ*), Weeks (Heb.: *shabu'oth*), and Tabernacles (Heb.: *sukkoth*). The latter two were harvest feasts. The origin and the development of these observances are obscure and complex. The agricultural Feast of Weeks, better known as Pentecost, was the occasion of gratitude for the early harvest. The Feast of Tabernacles, also known as Ingathering, was the harvest festival in autumn for the fruits of the threshing floor and the winepress. It is called Tabernacles (or Booths) because the people lived in booths during the seven days of the festival observance.

A valuable nonbiblical source of information about the agricultural cycle in Palestine is the Gezer Calendar, a small, limestone plaque discovered by R. A. S. Macalister in 1908 during his excavations of Gezer, which is located eighteen miles northwest of Jerusalem. This agricultural calendar, now on exhibit in the Istanbul Archaeological Museum, dates to the late tenth century B.C.E. Written in Hebrew, it refers, in almost chronological order, to the months of the year according to the harvests associated with them. The Gezer Calendar may become a more valuable resource when uncertainties about its interpretation have been removed.

Rainfall

The Hebrew Bible is rich in vocabulary for "rain," with general agreement on the following distinctions. *Maṭar* signifies rain in general; *yoreh (moreh)* usually designates the early or first rain of autumn which softens the soil in preparation for plowing. *Geshem* ordinarily refers to the heavy rains between November and January. *Malqosh* is used for the later or spring rains in late March and early April. It is related to *leqesh* (Amos 7:1), meaning "late planting" of grain. Some think *leqesh* refers here to the crop that remained after the first mowing and belonged to the king. Private citizens would have been heavily dependent on access to this second crop.

Amos reports that one of the chastisements the Lord inflicted upon his people was drought: "And I also withheld the rain from you when there were yet three months to the harvest; I would send rain upon one city, and send no rain upon another city; one field would be rained upon, and the field on which it did not rain withered" (Amos 4:7).

On a more positive note, Hosea expresses poignantly Israel's longing for the divine presence, which is as assured as the annual cycle of rainfall: "Let us know, let us press on to know the LORD; his going forth is sure as the dawn; he will come to us as the showers, as the spring rains that water the earth" (Hos. 6:3).

Dew is mentioned frequently in the Bible in both literal and figurative senses. Because of the limited rainfall in Palestine, dew is indispensable for the continuing growth of vegetation. During the summer months when rain is lacking, the dew is plentiful. The metaphorical uses of dew are multiple. Dew signifies the divine renewal of Israel's life: "I [the LORD] will be as the dew to Israel" (Hos. 14:5). Micah sounds the same note when he speaks of Israel's positive influence on humanity: "Then the remnant of Jacob shall be in the midst of many peoples like dew from the LORD, like showers upon the grass" (Micah 5:7). Hosea uses dew figuratively to describe what is ephemeral. Israel's love of God is disappointingly fleeting: "What shall I [the LORD] do with you, O Ephraim? What shall I do with you, O Judah? Your love is like a morning cloud, like the dew that goes early away" (Hos. 6:4). Once the sun rises, the dew disappears; so too Israel's love of God. In passing a verdict on the transitoriness of the people of Israel and their idols, Hosea's Lord says: "Therefore they shall be like the morning mist or like the dew that goes early away, like the chaff that swirls from the threshing floor or like smoke from a window" (Hos. 13:3).

Natural Scourges

The word "sirocco," derived from Arabic *sharq* ("east") through Italian *scirocco,* designates a warm, dust-laden east wind off the desert. It usually blows in autumn and spring and is accompanied by devastating heat; it may last several days and can be destructive. In the context of Israel's impending doom in the reign of King Hoshea (732–724 B.C.E.), Hosea uses the east wind metaphorically for the Assyrians, who will invade Israel. He threatens: "Though he [Samaria] may flourish as the reed plant, the east wind [sirocco], the wind of the LORD, shall come, rising from the wilderness; and his fountain shall dry up, his spring shall be parched; it shall strip his treasury of every precious thing" (Hos. 13:15).

Among other natural scourges in Palestine are blight and mildew, which also cause crop failure. As a result of blight, caused by the scorching east wind, the crops become discolored and wither. Mildew, the destructive work of worms, has about the same effect on the grain. The Lord used these natural disasters as a warning to the unfaithful people of Israel, but they failed to heed the signs: " 'I smote you with blight and mildew; I laid waste your gardens and your vineyards; your fig trees and your olive trees the locust devoured; yet you did not return to me,' says the LORD" (Amos 4:9).

Threshing

The Bible mentions threshing frequently, because grain was a staple in the people's diet. Sometimes threshing is to be understood metaphorically, meaning the cruel treatment meted out to a conquered enemy. Oftentimes threshing is to be taken literally, as the process of separating the kernels of grain from the straw stalks and husks. This can be done in several ways: by beating the stalks with sticks; by cattle trampling out the grain with their hooves; by cattle dragging a heavy sledge over the stalks, the underside fitted with sharp stones or iron points. A sledge is an instrument consisting of a wooden platform turned up slightly in the front and weighted with stones.

Micah utilizes the second method in the figurative sense when describing the restoration of Jerusalem amidst threats from neighboring nations: "But they do not know the thoughts of the LORD, they do not understand his plan, that he has gathered them as sheaves to the threshing floor. Arise and thresh, O daughter of Zion, for I will make your horn iron and your hoofs bronze; you shall beat in pieces many peoples, and shall devote their gain to the LORD, their wealth to the Lord of the whole earth" (Micah 4:12–13). God is the harvester, and

Jerusalem (Zion) the beast treading on the sheaves. The attacking nations bent on the conquest of Jerusalem would themselves be vanquished.

Amos refers to the third method of threshing in two well-known sections. Passing judgment on the nations, Amos indicts Aram (Syria) "because they have threshed Gilead with threshing sledges of iron" (Amos 1:3). Under King Hazael (842–806 B.C.E.), Syria devastated Gilead, located east of the Jordan River, and then usurped its territory from Israel. In his judgment against Israel, Amos, quoting the Lord, threatens, "Behold, I will press you down in your place, as a cart full of sheaves presses down" (Amos 2:13). Despite uncertainty about the exact meaning of the Hebrew verb in this metaphor, the imagery is quite clear.

The threshing floor on which the stalks were laid out was a flat, hard surface of rock or pounded earth, located in a high place with exposure to the wind. After the grain was harvested in the spring season, the actual threshing would continue through the summer months. The next step was the winnowing, accomplished by tossing the threshed grain into the air against the prevailing wind, which would carry off the light chaff, with the heavier grain falling to the ground. The sieving process followed the winnowing in order to remove any remaining foreign material. A sieve with a large mesh would retain such debris as stones and straw, while it would let the grain fall through to the ground.

Amos uses the metaphor of the sieve in an announcement of punishment: "For lo, I [the LORD] will command, and shake the house of Israel among all the nations as one shakes with a sieve, but no pebble shall fall upon the earth" (Amos 9:9). In other words, God would not annihilate; the faithful would be spared, but the sinner (the "pebble") would be purged.

Alluding to the harvest festival (*sukkoth*) in honor of Baal, Hosea commands, "Rejoice not, O Israel! Exult not like the peoples; for you have played the harlot, forsaking your God. You have loved a harlot's hire upon all threshing floors" (Hos. 9:1). Israel was guilty of apostasy (lustful acts) during the harvest festivities which took place on the threshing floor. Employing threshing, plowing, and harrowing (pulverizing and smoothing the soil) in the figurative sense, Hosea depicts the Lord's expectations of the Northern Kingdom: "Ephraim was a trained heifer that loved to thresh, and I spared her fair neck; but I will put Ephraim to the yoke, Judah must plow, Jacob must harrow for himself" (Hos. 10:11). In the prophet's view, the heifer had previously threshed unmuzzled and unencumbered by a wagon. Now the animal would be yoked to perform the more difficult chores of plowing and harrowing. This verse implies that Israel was faithful in the wilderness when conditions were congenial but not so in the Land of Canaan when the situation was more demanding.

Tools

Foretelling the new age of universal peace in a classic verse which he shares with Isaiah (2:4), Micah states, "And they shall beat their swords into plowshares, and their spears into pruning hooks" (Micah 4:3). Important as this verse is as a call for disarmament, it is of immediate interest for the information it provides about the primitive agricultural tools into which the weapons of war were to be converted. The Hebrew *hereb,* translated "sword," may really be a dagger. Excavations throughout the Near East have yielded countless daggers from the Bronze and Iron ages. "Plowshare" usually designates a cutting instrument of iron; it implies a moldboard type of plow that turns a furrow. This kind of instrument apparently did not exist in Iron Age Palestine. "Plowpoint" would be a more accurate translation. The eighth-century prophets knew only the metal-tipped scratch plow. Micah is referring to a wooden stick with a small metal point, drawn by oxen. Before the tenth century B.C.E. when iron became available to Israel, plowpoints were of copper or bronze. They penetrated the surface of the ground only about five inches, so deep plowing was impossible. In other words, plowpoints only broke up the soil, aerating and loosening it, without turning it over.

A spear was a long wooden shaft on which was mounted a head of stone or metal. Originating as early as 130,000–43,000 B.C.E., during the Middle Paleolithic period, it is described as a long stabbing sword (see chapter 3). A pruning hook was simply a blade attached to a handle, utilized in cutting back superfluous growth, like twigs and vines. The picture in Isa. 2:4 and Micah 4:3 is reversed in Joel 3:10: "Beat your plowshares into swords, and your pruning hooks into spears." The iron in the plowpoint or sword was valuable in itself; it was not an inexpensive, plentiful commodity. So when the militia was called up, the farmer had the smith convert the small piece of iron into a weapon; then, when peace was restored, the farmer had it transformed into an agricultural tool.

Plants

Plant life, whether cultivated or occurring naturally, forms a considerable part of the setting of the Bible and of the images drawn upon by the eighth-century prophets. Despite the abundant references to flora in the Bible, much remains to be known about the plants, trees, and flowers in biblical times. Certain Hebrew terms that are used to identify biblical flora are doubtful or ambiguous. This uncertainty can be explained in part by the long oral tradition lying behind the text. Also, some plants simply have been misidentified, designations have been equivocal, or the meanings of certain botanical terms have been forgotten. Modern Arabic is useful in identifying flora, because it has preserved some of the agricultural tradition of the Bible. Translations into English or other modern European languages, on the other hand, can compound the problem by applying anachronistically modern names to biblical flora.

One of the positive steps toward the identification and preservation of biblical flora was the establishment in Israel of Neot Kedumim, the 550-acre Biblical Landscape Reserve. Described as "a living museum of the wild and cultivated landscapes of biblical Israel," Neot Kedumim is located midway between Jerusalem and Tel Aviv in the Modiin region. Still in the process of development, this reserve, established in the 1970s, is dedicated to the study of nature in the Bible. Its goal, according to resident botanist Nogah Hareuveni, is to revive in their natural settings all the plants mentioned in the Bible and the Talmud. To date, over eighty thousand trees and saplings have been planted at Neot Kedumim.

Moses described Canaan as "a land of wheat and barley, of vines and fig trees and pomegranates, a land of olive trees and honey" (Deut. 8:8). This verse is a good partial summary of the material to be considered under biblical flora. A discussion of biblical plants, with specific reference to the eighth-century prophets, includes the following three categories: grains, fruits, and forest trees and shrubs. The trees and vines were ordinarily planted on terraces, and the cereals were sown in the valleys.

Grains

Wheat (Heb.: *ḥiṭṭah*), one of the principal crops of ancient Palestine, could be cultivated almost everywhere in the country and was harvested in the spring. In addition to being an important grain for food, wheat was an item of trade in good years. Used in the form of finely ground flour for baking breads and cakes, wheat was also presented to God as a cereal offering. Amos inveighs against the greedy merchants who defraud the poor by selling them an inferior product, designated "the refuse of the wheat" (Amos 8:6), that is, a mixture of chaff and debris left over from winnowing.

Another important grain in the Bible was barley (Heb.: *se'orah*). Cultivated as a winter crop, it was harvested about May. Cheaper than wheat and coarser, barley was considered a kind of second-rate food, used for feeding animals and the lower classes. Barley was used as a medium of exchange, as in Hosea: "So I bought her [Gomer] for fifteen shekels of silver and a homer and a lethech of barley" (Hos. 3:2). A homer is about six and a half bushels; a lethech, about three bushels. Barley too was used as a cereal offering to God.

Fruits

Among the fruit trees mentioned by the eighth-century prophets are the fig, olive (see chapter 6), sycamore, and vine. As today, the fig tree (Heb.: *te'enah*), a favorite, was important for life in biblical times. It is known for its beauty and the shade quality of its palm-shaped leaves. The fig tree produces two crops: the winter figs, which are inedible, and the edible summer figs. In a proverbial prediction about the peace, prosperity, and security to be enjoyed for a long time by the restored community of Jerusalem, Micah states, "But they shall sit every man under his vine and under his fig tree, and none shall make them afraid; for the mouth of the LORD of hosts has spoken" (Micah 4:4).

Speaking pessimistically because no upright person can be found in the land, Micah compares himself to a disappointed gleaner: "Woe is me! For I have become as when the summer fruit has been gathered, as when the vintage has been gleaned: there is no cluster to eat, no first-ripe fig which my soul desires" (Micah 7:1). The "first-ripe fig," the early green fig, is the most delicious of the fruit.

The people of Israel had been warned through natural disasters about impending doom, as Amos reminds them: "Your fig trees and your olive trees the locust devoured" (Amos 4:9). In describing Israel's impending punishment, Hosea, quoting the Lord, threatens, "And I will lay waste her vines and her fig trees" (Hos. 2:12). As part of the Lord's judgment on the people, the vines and fig trees will be turned into briars and thickets.

Recalling the idolatry the Israelites committed by consecrating themselves to the god "Baal of Peor" (Num. 25:1–5), Hosea, quoting the Lord, says, "Like grapes in the wilderness, I found Israel. Like the first fruit on the fig tree, in its first season, I saw your fathers. But they came to Baal-peor, and consecrated themselves to Baal, and became detestable like the thing they loved" (Hos. 9:10). In other words, the Lord's first encounter with Israel was as delightful as the experience of the weary traveler who chances upon an abundance of grapes in the wilderness or the farmer who discovers the first figs on the tree. But, then, the people's apostasy alienated the Lord and led to disastrous consequences.

In a vision, God shows Amos a symbolic basket of ripe summer fruit which spells inevitable doom. Amos makes this point by playing on two Hebrew words, which may have been pronounced the same way in the Northern Kingdom, *qayiṣ* (summer fruit) and *qeṣ* (end): "And he [the LORD] said, 'Amos, what do you see?' And I said, 'A basket of summer fruit *(qayiṣ).*' Then the LORD said to me, 'The end *(qeṣ)* has come upon my people Israel; I will never again pass by them' " (Amos 8:2). "Summer fruit" probably designates ripe figs, also pomegranates, and other perishable fruit that ripens during the summer.

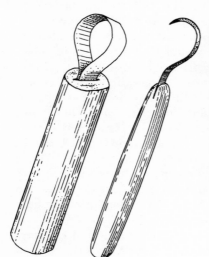

Knives for gashing sycamore figs in Egypt. Cutting hard, green sycamore figs to induce ripening was an ancient technique that is still used in modern times. The gashing of the fruit hastens the ripening process by increasing the ethylene production. (*J. Galil, "An Ancient Technique for Ripening Sycamore Fruit in East-Mediterranean Countries,"* Economic Botany 22 *[1968]:179–190; courtesy of The New York Botanical Garden; drawing by Douglas Gilbert*)

The sycamore tree (Heb.: *shiqmim*) is not to be confused with the North American sycamore, a plane tree, nor with the English maple tree, with which it has nothing in common. The biblical sycamore grows only in the lowlands and coastal plains, protected from the frost. A type of fig tree, it bears fruit several times a year. Although its fruit is smaller and inferior in quality to the common fig, it has always been an important item of food for the poor. The sturdy sycamore of the Bible may attain a height of over thirty feet, and its trunk may be three to six feet in diameter. Because the sycamore's wood is light and durable, it has been used widely in construction.

The best-known reference to the sycamore tree appears in Amos 7:14, where the prophet describes himself to Amaziah, the priest of Bethel, as "a herdsman, and a dresser of sycamore trees *(boles shiq-*

mim)." This second occupation refers to gashing, a technique for inducing the sycamore figs to ripen. At an early stage the figs are split open with a special knife, and several days later the gashed fruit is ripe and ready to be eaten. The gashing is called *balos* in Hebrew, and the only biblical reference to it is Amos 7:14.

The question is often asked how Amos could be "a herdsman, and a dresser of sycamore trees" at the same time. Hareuveni, keeper of Neot Kedumim, the Biblical Landscape Reserve, offers a plausible explanation. He relates that at the end of summer the shepherds moved their goats and sheep to the Jordan Plain in the Jericho Valley, an area flourishing with forage during the summer months. This was the season when unripe sycamore fruit covered the tips of branchlets. The fruit had to be pierced and then wiped with oil if it was to ripen. This time-consuming process was done in Amos' day, but it is not done today because the time and labor involved would make the marketing of the fruit too expensive. In exchange for grazing rights for their flocks, the shepherds dressed the sycamore fruit.

Hareuveni speculates that in the Jericho Valley, Amos had the opportunity of meeting the shepherds from Bethel, from whom he learned of the rampant injustices abroad in the Northern Kingdom. His explanation helps in understanding how Amos earned his livelihood both by shepherding and by piercing sycamore fruit. At the same time, it explains in part how Amos knew of events that were happening in Samaria.[2]

As idyllic as this explanation may be, it is speculative. In the opening verse of the Book of Amos he is described as a *noqed,* probably a wealthy landowner and farmer, so Amos may not have been a simple shepherd on hired land.

Growing grapes is one of the oldest forms of agriculture. The grapevine (Heb.: *gephen*) is as characteristic of ancient Israel as the fig and olive trees, although the grapevine demands greater care and requires more moisture and sun. It played an important role in the economic life of the people, many of whom had only their vineyards as a source of income. The Samaria ostraca shed some light on wine and oil in the economy of the eighth century B.C.E. Written in ancient Hebrew, these ostraca were, as already mentioned, administrative documents of some kind, perhaps labels for the jars of wine and oil or receipts for the delivery of wine and oil to the royal treasury.

Planted on the slopes of hills, the vine would either creep along the ground or climb trees; it often grows among the branches of fig trees. The planting and care of a vineyard (Heb.: *kerem*) is described in detail in Isaiah's Song of the Lord's Vineyard (Isa. 5:1–7). The harvesting of grapes (Heb.: *'anabim*) in August or September was the occasion for great vintage festivals, a time of celebration accompanied by song and dance.

Grapes may be eaten fresh or they may be dried into raisins. The Lord directs Hosea to buy back Gomer, his adulterous wife, and to love her, "even as the LORD loves the people of Israel, though they turn to other gods and love cakes of raisins" (Hos. 3:1). Cakes of raisins, a delicacy consisting of sun-dried grapes pressed into cakes, were used perhaps for offerings in pagan festivals.

Grapes may be pressed to juice or made into wine. Because of the scarcity of water, wine was a necessity of life. At Gibeon (modern el-Jib), six miles northwest of Jerusalem, archaeologists discovered an eighth- to seventh-century B.C.E. winery. Evidence of the Gibeon wine industry included over sixty vats cut into rock, a wine cellar, and wine jars. In addition to being consumed at meals, wine was used as a medicine as well as cultically in sacrifices and offerings.

A wine decanter. This vessel, known as a "water decanter," was common in Iron Age II. Globular in appearance and of light red ware, this Judahite decanter stood nine inches high, was seven inches in diameter, and had a capacity of two and a half quarts. *(N. Avigad, "Two Hebrew Inscriptions on Wine-Jars,"* Israel Exploration Journal 22 *[1972]:1–9; courtesy of Nahman Avigad; drawing by Douglas Gilbert)*

Wine was produced by means of a winepress, consisting of two vats cut into a rock at different levels, with a connecting channel from the upper to the lower level. The first pressing was accomplished by treading the grapes in the larger, higher vat; then the pressed-out juice would flow through the channel into the lower vat. The second pressing was done by means of a beam weighted with a stone. The fermentation process took place in the lower vat; when completed, the wine was stored in jars or skins. These wine vats could also have been used for making olive oil.[3]

Grape-growing is a rich source of imagery in the Bible, especially with the eighth-century prophets. The vine symbolizes peace, prosperity, and fertility. The vine was also a national symbol, as Hosea indicates: "Israel is a luxuriant vine that yields its fruit" (Hos. 10:1). Certainly, Israel had been blessed, but these blessings, as Hosea charges, led eventually to the downfall of God's people.

In an announcement of salvation concerning the restored community, Hosea, quoting the Lord, says of the people of Israel, "They shall blossom as the vine, their fragrance shall be like the wine of Lebanon" (Hos. 14:7) Rich agricultural metaphors are used, as here, to symbolize God's blessings: the vine flourished in Israel, and Lebanon was famous for its scented wine.

Concerning the use of wine in religious practice, Hosea makes some pointed observations. Indicting cultic excesses, he repeats a proverb: "Wine *(yayin)* and new wine *(tirosh)* take away the understanding" (Hos. 4:11). The distinction between these two Hebrew words is not sharp; sometimes they are used synonymously. True religion requires a sense of responsibility springing from sobriety.

Hosea rebukes the people of Israel for their participation in fertility rites directed to Baal. Quoting the Lord, he says, "For grain and wine they gash themselves, they rebel against me" (Hos. 7:14). Any form of laceration in the practice of religion was a perversion for Israel.

In a judgment speech about the impending exile, Hosea reminds the people of Israel that they will not have the opportunity to practice their traditional rituals in a foreign land: "They shall not pour libations of wine to the LORD; and they shall not please him with their sacrifices" (Hos. 9:4).

In a judgment against Israel, Hosea states, "Threshing floor and winevat shall not feed them, and the new wine shall fail them" (Hos. 9:2). Threshing floors and wine vats may be located together where bedrock comes to the surface of the ground. In the exile the threshing floor and wine vat will be unproductive, yielding nothing.

All the blessings of life, summarized in the phrase "the grain, the wine, and the oil," come from the Lord, not from Baal. When the people of Israel failed to acknowledge that fact, they were punished, as the prophet states: "And she [Israel] did not know that it was I [the LORD] who gave her the grain, the wine, and the oil. . . . Therefore I will take back my grain in its time, and my wine in its season" (Hos. 2:8–9). However, when the covenant is renewed through the Lord's initiative, the cycle of nature will be restored: "And the earth shall answer the grain, the wine, and the oil" (Hos. 2:22). The Lord will respond to the plea of "the grain, the wine, and the oil" when the relationship between God and Israel is restored.

On one occasion Hosea alludes to the adverse effects of intoxicants, observing, "On the day of our king the princes became sick with the heat of wine" (Hos. 7:5). Apparently, at a royal banquet during a festival, perhaps celebrating a coronation, some of the guests overindulged.

Amos also alludes to the adverse effects of wine when he says, "But you made the Nazirites drink wine" (Amos 2:12). The people of Israel had coerced the Nazirites to break their vow not to drink intoxicants. According to Num. 6:1–21, the Nazirites (meaning "consecrated" ones), as well as abstaining from liquor, did not use a razor on the body, nor did they have contact with the dead.

Amos also indicts the people for their perversion of religious rites: "And in the house of their God they drink the wine of those who have been fined" (Amos 2:8). During a religious ceremony in the very sanctuary of Israel they consume wine extorted from the poor.

In passing judgment on the people of Israel, Amos says, "You have planted pleasant vineyards, but you shall not drink their wine" (Amos 5:11). The fields where the vineyards were planted had been acquired fraudulently from small farmers. But after the redemption of Israel, "they [the people of Israel] shall plant vineyards and drink their wine" (Amos 9:14). Enjoying the fruit of one's labor is a symbol of peace and prosperity.

In a judgment speech, Micah indicts Judah: "You shall sow, but not reap; you shall tread olives, but not anoint yourselves with oil; you shall tread grapes, but not drink wine" (Micah 6:15). Blessings turn into curses when the whole agricultural cycle is unproductive. Micah's only negative reference to wine and other intoxicants is made sarcastically: "If a man should go about and utter wind and lies, saying, 'I will preach to you of wine and strong drink,' he would be the preacher for this people!" (Micah 2:11). In other words, the people apparently would give approval to the intemperate preacher.

Forest Trees and Shrubs

In a classic passage (later quoted in defense of Jeremiah when he was accused of blasphemy and treason for prophesying the destruction of Jerusalem and the Temple; Jer. 26:18), Micah foresees the destruction of Jerusalem and the Temple as an indictment of Judah's religious and political leadership: "Therefore because of you Zion shall be plowed as a field; Jerusalem shall become a heap of ruins, and the mountain of the house a wooded (*ya'ar*) height" (Micah 3:12). Although this prophecy has not been fulfilled literally, attempts have been made in history to do so. In this verse, as well as in Amos 3:4, "Does a lion roar in the forest *(ya'ar)*, when he has no prey?" *ya'ar*, the common Hebrew word for "forest," is used. Defined as wild, uncultivated land with permanent vegetation, forests in the biblical period were notable in Upper Galilee. As Amos suggests, wild animals inhabited the forests, and it may have been for this reason that forests, like the wilderness, intimidated people.

The cedar (Heb.: *'erez*), considered the prince of trees, is a magnificent mountain tree. It symbolizes many things, including pride, strength, prosperity, and security. This exalted tree may live as long as two thousand years and attain a height in excess of seventy feet, with its trunk measuring six to nine feet in width. The wood of this evergreen coniferous tree is so fragrant and durable that it has always been in demand for the construction of buildings and furnishings. The Temple in Jerusalem was constructed of cedar wood; likewise Solomon built his "House of the Forest of Lebanon" (part of his palace in Jerusalem) from imported cedar wood. An important item of trade, cedar wood was imported in large quantities by David and Solomon. The botanist Zohary summed up the qualities of the cedar tree by saying, "What the lion was to the animal world, the cedar was to the plant world."[4]

Reciting the "mighty acts of God" on behalf of Israel, Amos quotes the Lord: "Yet I destroyed the Amorite before them, whose height was like the height of the cedars, and who was as strong as the oaks; I destroyed his fruit above, and his roots beneath" (Amos 2:9).

The Book of Hosea ends on an idyllic note with a divine speech: "I will be as the dew to Israel; he shall blossom as the lily, he shall strike root as the poplar [or "Lebanon cedar"]; his shoots shall spread out; his beauty shall be like the olive, and his fragrance like Lebanon. They shall return and dwell beneath my shadow, they shall flourish as a garden; they shall blossom as the vine, their fragrance shall be like the wine of Lebanon. O Ephraim, what have I to do with idols? It is I who answer and look after you. I am like an evergreen cypress, from me comes your fruit" (Hos. 14:5–8).

The subject of this salvation oracle is the redemptive love of God, described in rich and colorful agricultural figures. The white lily (Heb.: *shoshannah*), grown in Galilee and on Mt. Carmel, is included here. It is the symbol of beauty and fertility. Lebanon is mentioned figuratively three times: the first alludes to the strength and permanence of the cedars, the second refers to the fragrance of the cedar wood, and the third concerns the superior reputation of Lebanon's wine. Lebanon denotes the mountain range that extends along the Syrian coast through modern Lebanon. In antiquity Lebanon was the homeland of the Phoenicians.

This same passage contains the Bible's only reference to God as a tree: "I am like an evergreen cypress (Heb.: *berosh*), from me comes your fruit" (Hos. 14:8). This tall evergreen, common in the Judean mountains, was used in the construction of buildings and furniture. The supply of evergreen cypress wood in Israel was adequate for local building requirements, so it did not have to be imported from Lebanon.

The oak (Heb.: *'allon* and *'elon*) is an acorn-bearing tree symbolizing strength, pride, and longevity. It too was used for construction, but it was also associated with sacrificial offerings: "They sacrifice on the tops of the mountains, and make offerings upon the hills, under oak (Heb.: *'allon*), poplar (Heb.: *libneh*), and terebinth (Heb.: *'elah*), because their shade is good" (Hos. 4:13). The people of Israel are accused of reverting to their habit of sacrificing on high hills and under green trees. The ample shade of these trees concealed not only cult practices but also ritual prostitution, as Hosea suggests sarcastically. Lawrence Stager suggests that these "green trees" at the peak sanctuaries may have been specially planted as sacred groves. Common in classical literature, sacred groves have been found at Kourion in Cyprus, the site of the sanctuary of Apollo Hylates, the god of the woodland, and at the Kition temple. Kition, a fortified town during the Late Bronze Age (1550–1200 B.C.E.), is on the south coast of Cyprus. At this site archaeologist Vassos Karageorghis uncovered a complex of temples. Between two of the temples were pits, wells, and channels which apparently constituted a sacred garden.

According to Zohary, *libneh* in this context is not to be translated "poplar" but "styrax," which is found together with the oak and the terebinth. The white poplar grows only in moist ground, not on mountaintops. The whitish color of the styrax's leaves accounts for its Hebrew name *libneh*, meaning "white." This is an example of the confusion caused by translators, in this case the Revised Standard Version, with respect to plant nomenclature. The terebinth, like the oak with which translators sometimes confuse it, is a mighty tree, also associated with cult practices. Attaining a height of thirty feet, it is easily recognized by its broad, spreading branches alluded to in Hos. 4:13. The olive tree will be discussed in chapter 6.

Thorns and Thistles

Zohary laments the great confusion surrounding the identification of the more than a hundred plants belonging to "thorns and thistles." Little consistency is evident in modern translations with respect to this category. The problem is understandable, however, because even today it is difficult for the ordinary person to distinguish various kinds of thorns and thistles.

The final chapter of Micah opens with a lament (Micah 7:1–7) that presents a pessimistic view of the times. The lonely prophet is surrounded by corruption and apostasy; no one can be trusted. He says, "The best of them is like a brier *(hedeq)*, the most upright of them a thorn hedge" (Micah 7:4). The *hedeq* is a thorny plant, often serving as a hedge to protect gardens from human and animal marauders; it is also used as fuel. This perennial shrub is common in Israel. It stands three to five feet high, with pink or blue flowers.

To frustrate Israel in its pursuit of apostasy, the Lord will erect obstacles along the way: "Therefore I will hedge up her way with thorns *(sirim);* and I will build a wall *(gader)* against her, so that she cannot find her paths" (Hos. 2:6). This verse may refer to the pathways of terraced slopes being obscured by thorns and new walls. *Sirim* are low shrubs of the rose family, used for fuel and fencing. This multi-branched shrub, one to two feet high, is the most common of its kind in Israel, especially in Jerusalem. Zohary describes this dwarf shrub as a "thorny burnet." *Gader* designates a fence built of stones, or stones and plants. Today, vineyards are still protected with stone fences topped with thorny shrubs (cf. Isaiah's Song of the Lord's Vineyard, Isa. 5:1–7).

According to Hareuveni, *"Seerim* [*sirim*] branches intertwine so the wind cannot easily blow them off the fence, especially when stones are placed over them to hold them down."[5] He describes two arrangements of these thorny shrubs topping stone fences. In one case, a corral, the shrubs surrounding an enclosure are positioned with their thorns pointing inward to prevent the sheep and goats from climbing out over the fence. In the other case, the shrubs are laid with their thorns facing outward to prevent the goats and sheep from climbing in over the fence and destroying the vineyard.

Describing the punishment of exile for the Northern Kingdom, Hosea paints a desolate picture of wild vegetation overrunning the people's dwellings and valued possessions: "Nettles shall possess their precious things of silver; thorns *(hoah)* shall be in their tents" (Hos. 9:6). *Hoah,* a thorny plant, is a general designation for thorns; it may be the golden thistle.

Hosea predicts as punishment for Israel's idolatry that the cult places will fall into disuse: "The high places of Aven [Bethel], the sin of Israel, shall be destroyed. Thorn and thistle *(dardar)* shall grow up on their altars" (Hos. 10:8). Bethel, a royal shrine in the Northern

Kingdom, was the scene of debauchery. *Dardar* means "whorls"; as Zohary points out, the whorl-like leaves of the *dardar* distinguish it from other thorns and thistles.

Wormwood

Often a metaphor for bitterness and sorrow, and also for sin, wormwood (Heb.: *la'anah*) is a dwarf shrub sometimes used for healing in folk medicine. The plant is described as aromatic and bitter. The word "vermouth," a dry or sweet aperitif wine flavored with aromatic herbs, is derived from wormwood. Zohary relates that the Bedouin of the Sinai and the Negev use the dried leaves of wormwood in preparing tea. Amos mentions wormwood metaphorically in two places, when he inveighs against Israel's lack of justice. Injustice leads to great bitterness: "O you who turn justice to wormwood, and cast down righteousness to the earth!" (Amos 5:7). In the second case, Amos uses rhetorical questions in his attempt to show the people how unreasonable and absurd their conduct is: "Do horses run upon rocks? Does one plow the sea with oxen? But you have turned justice into poison and the fruit of righteousness into wormwood" (Amos 6:12). No, horses do not run upon rocks; the donkey is much preferred for cultivating hillside fields because it can nimbly negotiate the rocky slopes.

Flax

Both Hosea and the Gezer Calendar refer to flax (Heb.: *pishtah*). Flax is a fiber plant utilized in making linen. It is an annual, two or three feet high, with beautiful blue flowers; it grows on the coastal plain and in the Jordan Valley. In their perversity, the people of Israel thought Baal provided them with the staples of life; in fact, it was the Lord: "For she [Israel] said, 'I will go after my lovers, who give me my bread and my water, my wool and my flax, my oil and my drink' " (Hos. 2:5). Of the two materials for clothing mentioned here, each has a different source: the wool is pastoral, the flax agricultural.

Animals

The Israeli Nature Reserves Authority is playing the chief role today in the conservation and restoration of wildlife. Its objective is to restore to Israel every animal known to have inhabited Palestine in biblical times.

Hundreds of passages in the Bible refer to animals. Not counting synonyms, the Bible has about 120 names of animals, including mammals, birds, and reptiles. Among the leading scholars in this field, the following must be counted: the eighteenth-century Swedish botanist Carolus Linnaeus, the nineteenth-century British naturalist Henry B. Tristram, and the twentieth-century Israeli zoologist Friedrich S. Bodenheimer. Linnaeus framed rules for assigning names to plants and animals. His classification of animals, known as the Linnaean system, consists of the following: mammals, birds, reptiles, fishes, insects, and worms. The classification of animals used in this section of the present work is based on Bodenheimer's adaptation of Linnaeus.

The task of naming, classifying, and describing the animals of the Bible is exceedingly difficult because of ignorance about the natural history of Palestine. There are many divergent views about the identification of biblical animals; names attributed to certain animals in the past have often been inaccurate. Lacking knowledge of animals in Palestine, translators and commentators have misinterpreted the animal names in the Bible or have confused the animals of Palestine with similar species known to them from their homeland.

We will discuss the following, mentioned by the eighth-century prophets: domestic animals, wild animals, birds, reptiles, and insects.

Domestic Animals

Horse

In biblical times the horse was used for war, transportation, and hunting, but not for agriculture. The horse was most commonly used in warfare (see chapter 3). For several reasons the people of Israel were opposed to using horses. Symbolic of power and luxury, the horse was associated with the nobility of Palestine and neighboring countries. Also, to rely on horses for victory in war was to compromise God's role. In fact, the Hebrews were forbidden to amass horses (Deut. 17:16). Nevertheless, from the time of David and Solomon horses were in common use in Palestine, not as cavalry but with chariots.

In a prophecy of salvation about Jerusalem's being spared from Assyrian attack in 701 B.C.E., it is clear that the Lord does not need the military for victory: "But I will have pity on the house of Judah, and I will deliver them by the LORD their God; I will not deliver them by bow, nor by sword, nor by war, nor by horses, nor by horsemen" (Hos. 1:7). In another salvation oracle Hosea states that Israel has finally learned about the futility of making alliances with Assyria and of trusting in the war chariots of Egypt: "Assyria shall not save us, we will not ride upon horses" (Hos. 14:3).

Cattle

"Cattle" (Heb.: *baqar*) is a generic or collective term for ruminant animals, that is, animals that chew the cud. Known by many names, cattle are important in the Bible. The bull, symbol of strength and fecundity, played an important role in religion, as a divine symbol and as a sacrificial animal (see chapter 4). Oxen pulled the plow and dragged the sledge around the threshing floor. The cow was used for sacrifice and not primarily for dairy purposes.

Israel resisting God is compared to a stubborn heifer (a cow that has not calved). At times Israel was not amenable to being taught, just as a bucking heifer is unwilling to be led: "Like a stubborn heifer (*parah*), Israel is stubborn; can the LORD now feed them like a lamb in a broad pasture?" (Hos. 4:16).

As noted in the section "Threshing," in the wilderness Ephraim (Israel) was a docile heifer, enjoying the good life; in Canaan more was expected: "Ephraim was a trained heifer (*'eglah*) that loved to thresh. . . . But I will put Ephraim to the yoke" (Hos. 10:11). In this verse the Hebrew word for "heifer" is *'eglah*, designating a sacrificial animal when used in the literal sense, but here it is intended figuratively. In these verses Hosea uses different words for "heifer." As a farmer, he may have known a distinction that escapes present-day zoologists; then again, it may simply be poetic oration.

Perhaps the best-known reference to cattle in the Prophets is Amos' "cows of Bashan": "Hear this word, you cows of Bashan, who are in the mountain of Samaria, who oppress the poor, who crush the needy" (Amos 4:1). Amos uses the epithet "cows (*parot*) of Bashan" to describe the pampered, indolent women of Bashan, the lush region east of the Sea of Galilee. The fertility of Bashan with its fatted livestock is proverbial. These women condoned the patent injustices perpetrated by the Samaria residents against the poor. Some commentators understand "cows" as a cultic title applied to the women of Bashan, not simply a reference to their self-indulgence, in view of the fact that Yahweh is portrayed as a "bull." Also, "cows" may be an honorific title interpreted ironically by Amos. In his study "Animal Names as Designations in Ugaritic and Hebrew," Patrick Miller concludes that animal names may be used metaphorically as titles for leaders or nobles. In Amos 4:1 the feminine plural form *parot* ("cows") refers to the wives of leaders.[6]

Sheep

The fact the Bible has over five hundred references to sheep and lambs indicates their importance for the economy, especially for meat

Stele from Marash. An eighth-century B.C.E. Hittite stele from Marash, in Southern Turkey, shows two women in elegant garments and cylindrical hats sitting on chairs, with a small offering table between them. The one on the left holds a cup in one hand and a pomegranate in the other; the figure on the right holds a mirror and a pomegranate. This opulent scene suggests the luxury that surrounded such indolent, aristocratic women. *(Courtesy of the Museum of the Ancient Orient, Istanbul; drawing by Douglas Gilbert)*

and wool. The lamb, too, was the principal sacrificial victim. Hebrew is rich in vocabulary for these animals. In addition to the literal meaning, sheep and lambs are common symbols for innocence, gentleness, and the other passive virtues. In a salvation oracle describing Israel as a mighty remnant among the nations, sheep serve as a metaphor of the defenseless nations: "And the remnant of Jacob [Israel] shall be among the nations, in the midst of many peoples, like a lion among the beasts of the forest, like a young lion among the flocks of sheep" (Micah 5:8). Another salvation oracle, looking to a time of restoration, uses the analogy of the shepherd leading the flock: "I will surely gather all of you, O Jacob, I will gather the remnant of Israel; I will set them together like sheep in a fold, like a flock in its pasture" (Micah 2:12).

Wild Animals

Bear

The Syrian bear was fairly common in biblical times, especially in the hilly, wooded regions of Palestine. The herdsman Amos knew that the bear could be dangerous when upset or hungry. Describing the "day of the Lord" as a day of inescapable doom for an unfaithful nation, Amos uses this analogy: "As if a man fled from a lion, and a bear met him" (Amos 5:19), the biblical version of "going from the frying pan into the fire," according to one commentator. Apparently the lion is less of a threat than the bear, because the lion is more predictable.

In an announcement of punishment for Israel's infidelity, Hosea heightens the violence and fury of the situation by figurative use of the lion, the leopard, and the bear, frequent symbols of cruelty but also symbols of strength and agility in other contexts: "So I [the Lord] will be to them [Israel] like a lion, like a leopard I will lurk beside the way. I will fall upon them like a bear robbed [literally, "bereaved"] of her cubs, I will tear open their breast, and there I will devour them like a lion, as a wild beast would rend them" (Hos. 13:7–8). A bear is particularly aggressive if one tries to rob her cubs or interfere with her young.

Lion

The most feared of all animals, the lion was common in Palestine during biblical times; now the lion has completely disappeared from the Middle East. The Hebrew Bible uses at least six words for "lion,"

The "Shema" seal. Dating to the eighth century B.C.E., this seal belonged to "Shema," whose name appears in Hebrew script above the roaring lion. The writing below the lion identifies Shema as "servant of Jeroboam": that is, Jeroboam II, king of Israel. This finely executed seal from Megiddo furnishes evidence not only of the presence of lions in ancient Israel but also of the high level of material culture achieved in Iron Age II. The photograph is of a modern bronze cast of the original jasper seal, which is now lost. (*Courtesy of the Israel Department of Antiquities; photo by David Harris, Israel Museum, Jerusalem*)

the most frequent being the general term *'ari* (*'aryeh*). No wild animal is so often mentioned in the Bible as the lion. This awesome beast, cited about 135 times in the Bible, often serves as a metaphor symbolizing destruction, power, or ferocity.

Although the Bible makes no mention of it, lion-hunting, depicted on Assyrian reliefs, was a favorite sport of kings in ancient times. On the basis of lion-shaped weights, which bear the inscription "of the king," the lion may have been considered a royal beast in the late Assyrian period. Lions were used as decorative motifs on furniture in Solomon's Temple and the king's palace. A famous seal from the eighth century B.C.E., engraved vividly with the figure of a standing and roaring lion, was found at Megiddo by the excavator Gottlieb Schumacher in 1904. The inscription on this jasper scaraboid reads: "[Belonging] to Shema, [the] Servant [of] Jeroboam," referring to Israel's king Jeroboam II (786–746 B.C.E.).

As a herdsman, Amos had personal knowledge of the habits of the animals in Palestine. His first sermon contains several references to the lion. Justifying his right to speak out on the basis of a divine call, Amos cites incidents exemplifying the principle that nothing happens without a cause: "Does a lion roar in the forest, when he has no prey? Does a young lion cry out from his den, if he has taken nothing?" (Amos 3:4). The lion roars as it leaps on the prey; when the cubs in the lair are satisfied, they cry out. As the roaring of the lion inspires fear, so "the LORD roars from Zion" (1:2). Amos continues: "The lion has roared; who will not fear? The Lord GOD has spoken; who can but prophesy?" (3:8). No one can resist the challenge of God's word; the prophet is compelled to speak.

To indicate that only a small portion of Israel would be saved, Amos quotes a familiar saying (Heb.: *mashal*, "proverb"): "Thus says the LORD: 'As the shepherd rescues from the mouth of the lion two legs, or a piece of an ear, so shall the people of Israel who dwell in Samaria be rescued, with the corner of a couch and part of a bed'" (Amos 3:12). When one of the flock had been seized and ravaged by a lion, the shepherd, to clear himself of suspicion, had to produce evidence from the bloody remains of the carcass that the animal had actually been killed.

Hosea too has several references to the lion. Speaking as God's mouthpiece of Israel's return home at the end of the exile, he predicts: "They shall go after the LORD, he will roar like a lion; yea, he will roar, and his sons shall come trembling from the west" (Hos. 11:10). In the context of God's redeeming love the lion's roar, usually indicative of danger or wrath, symbolizes in this verse the lion's reassuring call to its mate or cubs.

In the context of the Syro-Israelite war (735–734 B.C.E.), when Israel formed a coalition with Syria against the king of Judah, who in turn sought protection from Assyria, Hosea quotes the Lord's formidable words: "For I will be like a lion to Ephraim, and like a young lion to the house of Judah. I, even I, will rend and go away, I will carry off, and none shall rescue" (Hos. 5:14). Like a voracious lion, the Lord will exercise moral judgment by annihilating both the Northern Kingdom of Israel (Ephraim) and the Southern Kingdom of Judah.

As already mentioned, Micah describes Israel, God's remnant, as a ravaging lion in relation to the defenseless nations, depicted here as sheep: "And the remnant of Jacob [Israel] shall be among the nations, in the midst of many peoples, like a lion among the beasts of the forest, like a young lion among the flocks of sheep, which, when it goes through, treads down and tears in pieces, and there is none to deliver" (Micah 5:8).

Leopard

Hebrew *namer* designates the spotted leopard and also the panther; they are synonymous. "Leopard" is derived from two Greek words: *leōn* ("lion") and *pardos* ("panther"). The strongest of the predatory animals in Israel, it is yellowish in color, with black spots; or it may be completely black. Its spotted coat serves as a camouflage, enabling the animal to hide even in the open. The Sinai leopard, described as the "great spotted cat," still exists in Israel. A leopard has been seen at En-gedi, the unique desert oasis lying between the shore of the Dead Sea and the arid Judean desert. Enriched by an abundance of fauna (animals) and flora (plants), as well as fresh water, En-gedi today is a magnificent nature reserve. In addition to the leopard of En-gedi, it is estimated that as many as two dozen leopards may be lurking in Israel.

A Hellenistic building (182–175 B.C.E.), Qasr el-Abd, located at Araq el-Emir in the Wadi es-Sir of the Hashemite Kingdom of Jordan (Transjordan), was decorated with an animal fountain. Uncertain of the precise identification of the animal, the excavators described it generically as a feline. Sculptured in mottled red and white dolomite block, the beast has the appearance of a leopard rather than a lion. This sculpture was inserted in the lowest course of the building, with the animal's head serving as the water spout. Art historian Dorothy Hill made a detailed study of the feline adorning the Qasr el-Abd.[7] Identification of the beast vacillates between lion and leopard.

In an announcement of punishment, Hosea, likening God to a marauding leopard, describes the characteristic poise of this animal: "So

I [the LORD] will be to them [Israel] like a lion, like a leopard I will lurk beside the way" (Hos. 13:7).

Wild Ass

The wild ass, also known as the onager, is related to the horse, although the horse is larger and stronger. The wild ass, a native of southwest Asia, is a gregarious animal and travels in herds. The wild ass is often used figuratively in the Bible to symbolize gregariousness and stubbornness. Hosea compares stubborn Israel to a wild ass wandering off to Assyria: "For they [Israel] have gone up to Assyria, a wild ass *(pere')* wandering alone; Ephraim *('eprayim)* has hired lovers" (Hos. 8:9). In this verse Hosea puns on *pere'* and *'eprayim,* which sound alike in Hebrew. In the days of Hoshea (732–724 B.C.E.), last king of Israel, the Northern Kingdom paid tribute to Assyria; Hosea may be alluding to this act of vassalage on the part of Hoshea.

Birds

Dove

Hebrew *yonah* (Jonah), meaning "dove," derives, in the opinion of some, from a root indicating a moaning sound. The argument may find support in Isa. 38:14: "I moan like a dove." The dove is a common domestic bird, a large pigeon with long wings, designated in the Book of Leviticus as the appropriate sacrificial offering of the poor.

The dove is often considered silly for being too familiar with humans, thereby allowing itself to be trapped and domesticated. Inveighing against Israel's lack of diplomatic sense by seeking alliances with Egypt and Assyria, instead of trusting in God, Hosea quotes the Lord: "Ephraim [Israel] is like a dove, silly and without sense, calling to Egypt, going to Assyria. As they go, I will spread over them my net; I will bring them down like birds of the air" (Hos. 7:11–12).

According to Godfrey R. Driver, who wrote extensively on the birds of the Old Testament: "They [doves] are able to cover immense distances at great speed in search of food, a habit from which the homing instinct has been developed."[8] Hosea alludes to this trait when describing Israel's return from exile: "They shall come trembling like birds *(ṣippor)* from Egypt, and like doves from the land of Assyria; and I will return them to their homes, says the LORD" (Hos. 11:11). In this verse, *ṣippor* (a generic term for any small bird of the passerine kind, that is, songbirds of perching habits) is probably the sparrow, in contrast to the dove.

Vulture

Confusion exists about whether Hebrew *nesher* should be translated "eagle" or "vulture." According to Driver, *nesher* designates the griffon vulture rather than the eagle, although at least twenty-eight times it is translated "eagle." The griffon vulture is between three feet and four feet long, with a wingspan of almost eight feet. The white patch on its head gives the impression of baldness. The vulture, described as more gregarious than the eagle, is a carrion-eating (flesh unfit for food) bird; the eagle is the largest of all the birds of prey.

In a lament over Sennacherib's impending deportation of the people of Judah in 701 B.C.E., Micah quotes the Lord: "Make yourselves bald and cut off your hair, for the children of your delight; make yourselves as bald as the eagle [griffon vulture], for they shall go from you into exile" (Micah 1:16). Shaving the head was a sign of mourning.

At the approach of the Assyrians the Lord orders the battle alarm to be sounded: "Set the trumpet to your lips, for a vulture [*nesher*] is over the house of the LORD" (Hos. 8:1). The swift-swooping griffon vulture symbolizes the Assyrians descending on the land of Israel.

Ostrich (and Jackal)

The ostrich, a two-toed flightless fast runner, is the largest of birds, standing between six feet and eight feet tall and weighing up to three hundred pounds. Because of its beautiful plumage, the ostrich is sometimes referred to in Hebrew as *kenaph renanim*, questionably translated "Its wing rejoices." This expression is taken from Job 39:13, which is part of a passage describing the habits of the ostrich. Ostrich eggs were used for beads; decorated eggs have been found at Phoenician and Punic (relating to Carthage) sites. Considered a timid, stupid bird, the ostrich consumes almost anything without discriminating, and it makes little attempt to avoid being captured. The ostrich also symbolizes such unattractive human qualities as cruelty and uncleanness. With the introduction of the Ethiopian ostrich, this bird is once again present in Israel.

Addressing himself to Judah and Jerusalem, Micah wails over their inevitable fate, as one would mourn for the dead: "For this I will lament and wail; I will go stripped and naked; I will make lamentation like the jackals *(tannim),* and mourning like the ostriches *(bath ya'a-nah)"* (Micah 1:8).

In the Bible there appears to be a mistaken identity of the ostrich with the owl. The Hebrew term in question is *bath ya'anah,* meaning literally either "daughter of greed" or "daughter of the wilderness."

Driver translates the Hebrew expression as "eagle-owl," the largest of the owls. The owl is so secretive that little is known about it, except that it symbolizes deserted places and bad omens.

The jackal, classified as a wild mammal, is included here because it is often linked with the ostrich in descriptions of the wilderness. Jackals (*tannim*) are grayish brown and the size of a small dog. Living in packs near human settlements, they are scavengers. One of the most common mammals in Palestine, jackals usually move about at night. Their cry is described as a wailing howl, and they symbolize desolation.

Reptiles

Snake

Hebrew *nahash* is the generic name in the Bible for "snake," whether poisonous or nonpoisonous. "Snake" is preferred to "serpent," which is archaic. A contemptible creature representing potential danger in biblical literature, the snake is rarely perceived in a positive way. In the ancient Near East the snake was a symbol of the deity and of fertility. Jars and incense vessels decorated with snakes give evidence of a snake cult in early Palestine. At Dan, one of the two national sanctuaries of the Northern Kingdom, excavators uncovered a large storage jar decorated with a snake in relief. Now on display in the Israel Museum, this jar, dating from the tenth to the ninth century B.C.E., was found in a storage area adjacent to the "high place." At such sites as Gezer, Beth-shan, Beth-shemesh, Hazor, and Shechem, the snake-goddess Hathor was worshiped during the Early Iron Age.

To emphasize that the "day of the Lord" was to be a day of judgment, not victory, Amos uses the metaphor of the snake, capable of inflicting a poisonous bite with deadly results: "It is . . . as if a man . . . went into the house and leaned with his hand against the wall, and a serpent bit him" (Amos 5:18–19). Resting the hand near a snake could cause it to strike. The snake that Amos envisions was probably living in a mudbrick wall.

Describing his vision at the altar, Amos utilizes the metaphor of the sea monster to indicate that the Northern Kingdom cannot escape destruction: "And though they hide from my sight at the bottom of the sea, there I will command the serpent, and it shall bite them" (Amos 9:3). The mythical sea monster, subdued at creation, will carry out the divine command by biting the people of Israel as they try to escape divine judgment.

Employing the metaphor of the snake eating dust (Gen. 3:14), Micah predicts that the nations will be subdued: "They [the nations] shall lick

A cylindrical cultic stand at Beth-shan. Dating to the time of Pharaoh Rameses III (1182–1151 B.C.E.), this two-handled cultic object was found at Beth-shan, located between the Jezreel and Jordan valleys. Serpents coil up the sides from below, and doves are perched on the handles. Doves and serpents are commonly associated with Ashtoreth, the female consort of the Canaanite deity El. According to excavator Alan Rowe, this cultic stand was perhaps used in sacred rites associated with agriculture. *(A. Rowe,* The Four Canaanite Temples of Beth-Shan *[Philadelphia: University of Pennsylvania Press, 1940]; courtesy of the Israel Department of Antiquities and Museums)*

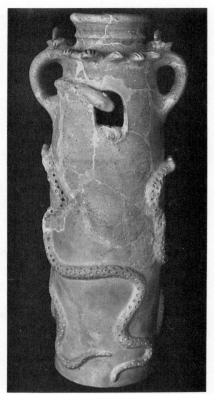

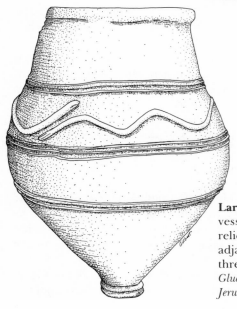

Large storage jar at Dan. This vessel, decorated with a snake in relief and found in a storage area adjacent to the "high place," is about three feet high. *(Courtesy of the Nelson Glueck School of Biblical Archaeology, Jerusalem)*

the dust like a serpent, like the crawling things of the earth" (Micah 7:17). "Crawling things" are hard to define, perhaps earthworms or a broader term. Whatever the specific reference, they are an effective symbol of the nations' humiliation.

Insects

Locust

The locust plays a prominent, though usually negative, role in the Bible. The most frequently mentioned insect in biblical literature, the locust is a symbol of devastation, as is attested by the eighth plague (Exodus 10) and by the prophet Joel (1:4–12). A locust swarm can completely ravage cultivated vegetation. To mention a positive aspect, the locust was a good source of protein, as John the Baptist knew

Hebrew seal with a locust. This seal, which dates from the eighth to seventh century B.C.E., is a scaraboid of reddish-white carnelian. The two-line inscription is in ancient Hebrew characters. The carved locust under the inscription is well executed. *(Courtesy of Nahman Avigad; drawing by Douglas Gilbert)*

(Matt. 3:4), and was eaten as a delicacy. The Old Testament has at least nine Hebrew words for "locust," the most frequent designation being *'arbeh.*

To bring Israel to repentance, God sent calamities in the form of natural disasters as warnings, but the warnings went unheeded: " 'Your fig trees and your olive trees the locust *(gazam)* devoured; yet you did not return to me,' says the LORD" (Amos 4:9).

The first of Amos' visions of God's judgment was in connection with the ravenous locust as an agent of God's vengeance: "Thus the Lord GOD showed me: behold, he was forming locusts *(gobay)* in the beginning of the shooting up of the latter growth" (Amos 7:1). *Gobay,* a synonym for *'arbeh*, is found elsewhere only in the Book of Nahum, where he speaks of the inevitable fall of the hated city of Nineveh: "Your princes are like grasshoppers *('arbeh)*, your scribes like clouds of locusts *(gobay)* settling on the fences in a day of cold—when the sun rises, they fly away; no one knows where they are" (Nahum 3:17).

The scarab, the dung beetle of Egypt, became a sacred symbol in antiquity. Stamp seals in the form of a scarab (beetle), fashioned in stone and engraved, are found frequently in Palestine. At least two Hebrew seals with representations of a locust have come to light. One is an inscribed scaraboid from Megiddo, discovered in 1929; the other was acquired more recently in Jerusalem. The latter, a scaraboid of reddish-white carnelian, has a two-line ancient Hebrew inscription as well as a carved locust. Dating to the eighth to seventh century B.C.E., this scarab is especially relevant for the study of Amos, because the word for "locust" inscribed on the scarab is *hgbh*, as in Amos 7:1. Nahman Avigad, Israeli authority on seals, reads the inscription as "Belonging to Azaryaw [son of] *hgbh*" (to be pronounced "Haggobeh" or "Haggebah").

Avigad comments: "Our seal is the first known instance among Hebrew and related seals where a name is accompanied by a pictorial illustration of its meaning. The locust obviously serves here as the emblem of the Haggobeh or Haggebah family."[9]

6

The *Marzeaḥ*:
Banquets and High Living

Woe to those who lie upon *beds of ivory*, and stretch themselves upon their couches, and eat lambs from the flock, and *calves from the midst of the stall;* who sing idle songs to *the sound of the harp*, and like David invent for themselves instruments of music; who drink *wine in bowls*, and anoint themselves with *the finest oils*, but are not grieved over the ruin of Joseph! Therefore they shall now be the first of those to go into exile, and the revelry (*marzeaḥ*) of those who stretch themselves shall pass away. (Amos 6:4–7)

This passage is one of Amos' sermons on the doom of Israel and its luxury-loving society. The specific object of his indictment is the *marzeaḥ*, often translated as "revelry" or "banquet," but overindulgence of several kinds is implied. Because the etymology of *marzeaḥ* is uncertain and much about the nature of this institution is still unknown, the Hebrew word is difficult to render accurately in English. The existence of the *marzeaḥ*, however, is well attested. In addition to Amos, the only other specific biblical reference to the *marzeaḥ* occurs in Jer. 16:5–9. These two rather enigmatic prophetic texts will be clearer after a general description of the *marzeaḥ*.

Often the *marzeaḥ* was a pagan ritual that took the form of a social and religious association. The term may denote the group of people who participated in the rite or the building where the rite took place. The occasion for the meeting could be joyful or sorrowful; sometimes the *marzeaḥ* was the setting for mourning rites consisting of eating and drinking. Whether sacred repasts or memorial meals, these feasts lasted several days and were accompanied by excessive drinking. Wealth and affluence apparently were prerequisites for participation in the *marzeaḥ*.

The purpose of the funerary aspect of the *marzeaḥ* was to offer consolation to those in mourning. By sharing food and drink with the mourners, participants offered solace and comfort. Scholars who em-

phasize the memorial aspect of the *marzeaḥ* understand it as a feast for
and with deceased ancestors or Rephaim, a proper name in the Old
Testament for the inhabitants of Sheol.

In his graphic description of personal loneliness Jeremiah mentions
the *marzeaḥ* as a mourning rite in which he was forbidden to take part.
Here he refers both to the funerary cult and to the place of the funerary
feast or wake. Jeremiah's absence from the *marzeaḥ* was to serve as a
warning to the nation of inevitable doom. He relates the event in these
words:

> For thus says the LORD: Do not enter the house of mourning (*bet
> marzeaḥ*), or go to lament, or bemoan them; for I have taken away
> my peace from this people, says the LORD, my steadfast love and
> mercy. Both great and small shall die in this land; they shall not
> be buried, and no one shall lament for them or cut himself or
> make himself bald for them. No one shall break bread for the
> mourner, to comfort him for the dead; nor shall any one give him
> the cup of consolation to drink for his father or his mother. You
> shall not go into the house of feasting to sit with them, to eat and
> drink. For thus says the LORD of hosts, the God of Israel: Behold,
> I will make to cease from this place, before your eyes and in your
> days, the voice of mirth and the voice of gladness, the voice of
> the bridegroom and the voice of the bride. (Jer. 16:5–9)

The *marzeaḥ* had a long history, extending from the fourteenth century B.C.E. through the Roman period. It was prominently associated
with the ancient Canaanite city of Ugarit (modern Ras Shamra) on the
coast of Syria as well as with Palmyra on the northern edge of the
Syrian desert about 120 miles northeast of Damascus. A library of texts
from Ugarit has furnished a wealth of information on the religion of
Canaan and Syria. Probably the site of biblical Tadmor, Palmyra
reached the height of its power and prosperity in the Late Roman
period (135–324 C.E.). The *marzeaḥ* at Palmyra took the form of a
funerary cult and consisted of the main elements enumerated by Amos
in his description of the *marzeaḥ*. During the fifteen hundred years
when the *marzeaḥ* was in vogue some changes inevitably occurred in the
manner of its observance.

Amos 6:4–7 is a clear description of the *marzeaḥ*, although many
commentators have failed to identify it as such. In denouncing those
who indulged in the *marzeaḥ*, Amos enumerates five components of this
revelry. His listing is not haphazard; it follows the traditional order of
elements in an ancient banquet, as known from other sources. For
example, the preparation of the meat always preceded the preparation
of the wine. Also, the rite of anointing, musical accompaniment, and
eating in a prostrate position were integral parts of the banquet scene.

After his description of the *marzeaḥ*, Amos appends an ominous note, which makes it clear that the indulgent people of Samaria were participating in a funerary cult. Predicting the destruction about to befall Samaria, he says:

> And if ten men remain in one house, they shall die. And when a man's kinsman, he who burns him, shall take him up to bring the bones out of the house, and shall say to him who is in the innermost parts of the house, "Is there still any one with you?" he shall say, "No"; and he shall say, "Hush! We must not mention the name of the LORD." (Amos 6:9–10)

Beds of Ivory

The first element of the *marzeaḥ* that Amos mentions is the beds of ivory. This, however, is not his first reference to ivory. Earlier, when describing the prosperity and ostentation of the people of the Northern Kingdom of Israel he spoke of the "houses of ivory" (Amos 3:15) in Samaria, the royal city of the Kingdom of Israel located at modern Sebastiyeh. Whenever the prophets of the eighth century mention Samaria they do so with bitterness. Like the "houses of ivory" in the city, Samaria was the symbol for the prophets not only of luxurious self-indulgence but also of pagan immorality and flagrant injustice. "Houses of ivory" is not to be understood literally; the epithet refers to domiciles adorned with sumptuous ivory paneling and to furniture decorated with elaborate ivory inlays. Another biblical example of *pars pro toto* ("part for the whole") is the "House of the Forest of Lebanon," a part of Solomon's palace in Jerusalem so named because of its three rows of fifteen cedar pillars and wallboards imported from Lebanon (1 Kings 7:2–5).

The carvers' marks on the fragmentary remains of the Samaria ivories make it clear that Amos is referring to ivory inlays and insets. To the prophets, especially Amos, such luxury was possible for the wealthy class only by exploiting the poor of the land. Here was a flagrant example of the social injustice against which they railed.

The subject of ivory has a long and fascinating history in the Near East, offering insights into the social, economic, and religious life of Israelite society in the eighth century B.C.E. Always a luxury item, ivory is still a highly prized objet d'art.

The principal source of commercial ivory is the elephant, the two main species being the African and the Asian. The Asian elephant is sometimes incorrectly identified as the Indian elephant. The African elephant is the larger of the two species and also the more active. Weighing as much as six tons, it is easily identified by its large ears.

Both the female and the male have tusks averaging six feet in length; a pair may weigh one hundred pounds. The ivory tusks evolved from the two upper incisor teeth; they continue to grow during the life of the elephant.

The Asian elephant is smaller, and only the males have tusks, averaging five feet in length, with a pair weighing about seventy pounds. These tusks serve many purposes; with them the elephant can move objects, uproot trees, and defend itself. A subspecies of the Asian elephant is the Syrian elephant which became extinct after the eighth century B.C.E. It may have been the source of ivory for the Phoenicians and the Syrians. Elephants are vegetarians and inhabit grassy plains or forests.

The ancient texts have several references to elephants, although the Old Testament has none. Assyrian and Egyptian sources of the fifteenth century B.C.E. mention elephant hunts taking place in North Syria in the vicinity of Carchemish, a prominent military and commercial center. Pharaoh Thutmose III (1490–1436 B.C.E.) described a hunt in which 120 elephants were killed for their ivory. The famous Black Obelisk (now in the British Museum, London) of the Assyrian monarch Shalmaneser III (859–825 B.C.E.) has a classic depiction of an Asiatic elephant. Pictured with tusks, this elephant is being led away by an attendant. In addition, the Black Obelisk is decorated with several scenes of monarchs offering tribute. In one scene the king of Musri (possibly Egypt or the region northwest of Assyria) offers animals, including elephants; in another scene, Jehu (842–815 B.C.E.), king of Israel, kneels in submission, with his face touching the ground, before Shalmaneser III.

Among the gifts presented to Assyrian king Tiglath-pileser III (745–727 B.C.E.) when Arpad, the capital of a Syro-Hittite kingdom, surrendered were elephant hides and ivories. Hezekiah (715–687 B.C.E.), king of Judah, sent elephant hides and ivory inlays to Sennacherib of Assyria as tribute when he invaded Judah and besieged Jerusalem in 701 B.C.E. Listed among Hezekiah's items of tribute are ivory (inlaid) couches, ivory armchairs, elephant hide, and elephant tusks. Later, in 218 B.C.E. the best-known reference to elephants is Hannibal's leading his army together with a number of elephants across the Alps into northern Italy.

The gradual disappearance of elephants in ancient times is to be explained apparently both by the extensive cultivation of land and by the increased demand for ivory. These reasons may account for the fact that elephants are not mentioned in the Old Testament.

There were at least two, perhaps three, schools of ivory in biblical times: North Syria, Phoenicia, and perhaps South Syria. Ivory carvings

The Black Obelisk. This stone monument dating to the reign of King Shalmaneser III was found at Nimrud, where it would have stood in a public area. The Black Obelisk depicts various nations bringing tribute to the king, including elephants from Musri, a region either in Egypt or northwest of Assyria. *(Courtesy of the Trustees of the British Museum)*

of the North Syrian school reflect a Canaanite-Mycenean tradition, with Egyptian influence almost completely missing. Ivories of this tradition are represented principally at Nimrud in northern Assyria, where thousands have been found. Nimrud, nineteen miles south of modern Mosul (in northern Iraq) on the bank of the Tigris River, is biblical Calah (Gen. 10:11–12), an ancient Assyrian city founded by Shalmaneser I in the thirteenth century B.C.E. These carved ivories may have been brought to Nimrud as booty from Syria; then again, the craftsmen could have been taken to Assyria as part of the transfer of populations.

In the middle of the last century (1845–1848) Austen Layard, pioneer archaeologist of Mesopotamia, discovered the Nimrud ivories in the magnificent Northwest palace of Ashurnasirpal II (884–860 B.C.E.), who made Calah his capital. This palace was restored by Assyrian king Sargon II (722–705 B.C.E.), who, after conquering Samaria, brought the booty to Calah. A century after Layard's excavations, Max Mallowan discovered additional carved ivories in the palace of Ashurnasirpal II.

The motifs on Phoenician ivories are clearly of Egyptian inspiration. Representing an adaptation of Egyptian traditions of art and mythological symbolism to Canaanite-Phoenician themes, they are easy to identify. The ivories of ancient Israel were made by Phoenicians. Found extensively at Samaria and Nimrud, they also were present at Arslan Tash, the site of ancient Hadatu in North Syria on the Euphrates, where a French expedition led by François Thureau-Dangin excavated in 1928. The ivories at Arslan Tash resemble the Samaria ivories both in time and style. Ivories found at Khorsabad also resemble the Samaria ivories. Khorsabad is the modern Iraqi village on the site of Dur Sharrukin, the magnificent capital of Sargon II.

Irene Winter, specialist in the ivories of the Near East, believes that South Syria, specifically Damascus, was an important source of ivory. Suggesting that there is a South Syrian style of ivory-carving, she maintains that Damascus is the origin of the majority of ivories from Samaria. She argues that geographically neither North Syria nor Phoenicia would have included Aram (Syria) or ancient Israel. Archaeologically, little is known about Damascus because of lack of excavation, but historically it is known that the Northern Kingdom of Israel had close ties to Aram (Syria) as well as to Tyre. For example, in the time of King Hazael (842–806 B.C.E.), Damascus carried on regular commerce with Samaria; the goods of one would have been sold in the bazaars of the other. Some would argue for the Damascus origin of ivory from Amos 3:12, an uncertain text, by reading "Damascus bed" in place of "part of a bed." To do so would be stretching Hebrew syntax.

Summarizing the characteristics of ivories in the two major Syrian and Phoenician groups, Winter states:

> Syrian-style ivories may be characterized by a greater sense of action, by squatter, more powerful proportions, and by more highly charged compositions, compared with the more quiescent, elegant, and slender figures harmoniously disposed in space of the contemporary Phoenician style.[1]

In ancient Israel the most significant collections of ivories were uncovered at Megiddo and Samaria, although the difference between the two collections is striking. At Megiddo, over three hundred ivory fragments dating from the beginning of the Iron Age (twelfth century B.C.E.) came from the palace's treasury room. Gordon Loud, director of the University of Chicago expedition to Megiddo in 1937 when the ivories were found, dated them from 1350 to 1150 B.C.E.

A well-known ivory plaque from Megiddo, dating from the time of Pharaoh Rameses III (1182–1151 B.C.E.), sheds light on several elements of the *marzeaḥ* as described by Amos, especially the lyre, the cup,

A Megiddo ivory. This ten-inch long ivory plaque with a composite scene is a model of Canaanite narrative art. Found at Megiddo, it dates to the twelfth century B.C.E. (*Courtesy of the Israel Department of Antiquities and Museums; copyright held by The Oriental Institute, University of Chicago; drawing by Douglas Gilbert*)

and the bowl. Reflecting Egyptian influence, it is Canaanite narrative art par excellence. The plaque is incised with two scenes, separated by a vertical row of three plants; one scene is festive, the other military. In the left register, the king or prince seated on a throne is celebrating a victory. With his right hand he raises a cup to his lips; in his left hand is a lotus flower, a symbol of royalty. A woman in Syrian dress stands before the enthroned king. A female musician plays on an asymmetrical lyre with nine strings. Behind the throne stand two servants flanking a large mixing bowl, probably containing wine. In the right register of this composite scene, a triumphant ruler returns from war: a soldier with shield and spear leads two circumcised prisoners, who are bound and naked; behind them is the king standing in his chariot.

Samaria, a royal city of the Kingdom of Israel and the capital of the Northern Kingdom, was strategically located on the summit of a hill, about thirty-five miles north of Jerusalem. Reaching its second—its first under Omri-Ahab—zenith in the time of Jeroboam II (786–746 B.C.E.), sometimes called the "ivory age," the city was besieged by the Assyrians and finally taken in 721 B.C.E. During the two excavations at Samaria, the first under George Reisner from 1908 to 1910, the other under John Crowfoot from 1931 to 1935, among the most significant discoveries were the ostraca, principally administrative documents dating to 735 B.C.E., and the ivory inlays. Fragments of ivories were uncovered by Reisner, but the larger hoard came from Crowfoot's dig. Both the ostraca and the ivories shed light on the economic and religious status of the Northern Kingdom of Israel. The fact that the ostraca contain proper names compounded with the god "Baal" points to religious influence from Phoenicia, the homeland of Jezebel, Ahab's queen.

Samaria yielded over five hundred ivory fragments, dating to either the ninth or the eighth century B.C.E., though the eighth seems more likely. The earlier date was suggested by a reference in 1 Kings 22:39 to the "ivory house" of Israel's king Ahab (869–850 B.C.E.). However, on the basis of comparison with parallel collections found in the Assyrian royal palaces at Nimrud, Arslan Tash, and Khorsabad, the eighth-century date (the time of Amos) is convincing. These ivories were probably brought as tribute or spoil to the Assyrian centers from Syria, Phoenicia, and perhaps from Israel, especially since an ivory plaque inscribed in Hebrew was found at Nimrud.

Ordinarily ivories can be dated with reasonable accuracy by the archaeological context in which they are found. But the Samaria ivories, described by the excavators as "small, fragile, discolored by fire and by soil," were also badly broken. The excavators report that they were discovered in a disturbed context, on the crest of a hill in traces of a burnt layer between some walls. In fact, Hellenistic (332–63 B.C.E.) remains were found beneath the ivory hoard. Ivory can be more difficult to date than common and more fragile artifacts because the value and the hardness of ivory guarantee it long life. Pottery, for example, is so easily broken that it is short-lived by nature, whereas the more durable ivory is apt to be handed on like an heirloom from one generation to the next.

Only 40 percent of the Samaria ivories have been published, but it is safe to say that most were not of local origin. On the other hand, the discovery of some unfinished ivories found at Samaria suggests that at least these were carved locally. The Egyptian motifs decorating the ivories point to a style originating in Phoenicia; that is, the motifs are Egyptian, but the presentation is Phoenician. Egyptian mythological symbolism on the Samaria ivories is evident in representations of various deities, such as Horus, Ra, Heh, Isis, Nephthys, and Osiris. The Egyptian motif had already been taken over and adapted by the Phoenicians, who were the conduits of most things Egyptian in the region. The pagan symbolism adorning the ivories may have outraged Amos as much as the affluence and luxury which the Samaria ivories represented. Phoenicia's strong influence on Samaria during Ahab's reign (869–850 B.C.E.) was weakened by the rebellion of Israel's king Jehu (842–815 B.C.E.); however, Phoenician influence continued to be felt in the Northern Kingdom.

The well-known crouching lions are judged to be the best of the ivory pieces from Samaria. They are carved in the round, that is, in full sculptured form, unattached to a background. Just as Amos and Hosea refer to the roar of the lions, these two lions represented with open mouths appear to be roaring. The slots in the backs of these identical lions indicate that they were probably attached to furniture as decoration.

Among the Egyptian motifs depicted on the ivory plaques of Samaria are Isis and Nephthys kneeling and facing each other. With their

Crouching lions. Less than two inches high and carved in the round (unattached to a background), these two roaring lions from Samaria are identical. *(Courtesy of the Israel Department of Antiquities and Museums)*

The striding sphinx. This ivory plaque from Samaria stands less than four inches high. The sphinx is the closest approximation in appearance to the cherubim of Solomon's Temple. *(Courtesy of the Israel Department of Antiquities and Museums)*

Lion and bull in combat. This miniature ivory from Samaria depicts a lion grappling with a bull. The protruding tongue of the bull conveys its intense suffering. Animal combat was a common motif in ancient Near Eastern art. *(Courtesy of the Israel Department of Antiquities and Museums)*

wings they protect a tree *(djed)*, the symbolic emblem of Osiris, standing between the two goddesses. Osiris and Isis were the parents of
Horus, and Nephthys was the sister of Isis. Harpocrates (Horus as a
child) depicted on a lotus also decorates a Samaria ivory. Some think
this scene was meant to be reminiscent of Moses floating down the
Nile. Osiris, Isis, and Horus formed a trinity of Egyptian gods. From
Samaria comes the kneeling Heh, the personification of infinite space,
bearing the symbols of long life and happiness.

Also well known from Samaria is the winged sphinx striding in a
lotus thicket. The sphinx, a mythological creature with a lion's body
and a human head, has a beardless face and wears the flattened double
crown of Egypt. In Egyptian art the sphinx represents the might of the
pharaoh. In biblical tradition the winged sphinxes were the prototypes
of the cherubim in the description of the "holy of holies" in Solomon's
Temple (1 Kings 6:23–28).

A lion grappling with a long-horned bull is another common motif
on ivories, including Samaria ivories. The extraordinary detail of the
Samaria plaque vividly illustrates the painful struggle of animals in
combat.

Fan-shaped Phoenician palmettes used to decorate walls or furniture were also carved on Samaria ivories. One such panel depicts a
vertical line of trees, each trunk terminating in a voluted (scroll-
shaped) capital crowned in turn by a fan-shaped palmette.

Perhaps the best-known motif in the Phoenician tradition of art,
certainly the most common of the Phoenician ivory motifs, is the
"woman at the window," depicted on ivory, stone, and bronze objects.
There is only one example at Samaria, but it appears frequently at
Nimrud and Khorsabad in Assyria, at Arslan Tash in Syria, and in
Cyprus. Adorned with an Egyptian wig or headdress, the woman peers
through a window within recessed frames overlooking a balcony balustrade (a low railing) supported by voluted (scroll-shaped) columns.
The Baba Bathra section of the Talmud describes these balustrade
windows as "Tyrian" (Phoenician), in contrast to the Egyptian window. Unlike the Egyptian window, which was obstructed by a grille or
supporting columns, the Tyrian window made it possible to poke one's
head through the opening. The Tyrian windows were in the upper
chambers where the women's quarters were located.

The "woman at the window" motif, without implying sacred prostitution, is not uncommon in the Old Testament. Jezebel, for example, looked out from a Tyrian-style window, perhaps located in
Ahab's palace, as she awaited the fateful arrival of Jehu speeding up
the Valley of Jezreel, bent on massacre (2 Kings 9). In the Song of
Deborah (Judges 5) the mother of Sisera, a Canaanite king defeated

"Woman at the window." A woman wearing an Egyptian headdress is depicted at a balustraded window. Dating to the eighth century B.C.E., this ivory plaque was found in the Northwest Palace at Nimrud, but it probably originated in Phoenicia. *(Courtesy of the Trustees of the British Museum)*

The Salamis bed. This restored ivory bed from Salamis dates to 800 B.C.E. Its bedhead is elaborately decorated: on top of the frame is a row of seventeen stylized lotus flowers, and the three panels are adorned with carved ivory plaques. *(Courtesy of the Department of Antiquities, Nicosia, Cyprus, Vassos Karageorghis, Director)*

by the Israelites, awaits his return from battle, peering through the window of the palace. As the Ark of the Covenant was entering the City of David (Jerusalem), Saul's daughter Michal looked down through the window and saw David dancing before the Ark (2 Samuel 6).

In his graphic description of the *marzeah*, Amos gives prominence to the beds of ivory; they are the first element he enumerates. These were couches decorated with ivory inlays where guests sprawled during the festivities. An excellent example of this furniture is the ivory bed found in the cemetery of Salamis in Cyprus. In 1966 Vassos Karageorghis carefully excavated Tomb 79 at Salamis, which he describes as the richest tomb on the island. Dating the bed to the eighth century B.C.E., Karageorghis believes that the Salamis ivories, similar to the Nimrud ivories, were not made locally but were imported from Phoenicia when Cyprus was dominated by the Assyrians (about 709 B.C.E.). The headboard of the Salamis bed had three panels of ivory plaques, decorated with Phoenician art bearing Egyptian subjects. On the upper frieze is a series of Heh figures, identical with friezes from Samaria and Nimrud; the middle frieze consists of plaques decorated with palmettes and the lotus; the lower frieze is ornamented with wingless male sphinxes. Another example of a bed in domestic use in Iron Age II is an extant clay model of a bed from Lachish. It is a couch with a raised end, but the material of the original is unknown.

Further light is shed on the *marzeah* by a relief from the North Palace at Nineveh, which depicts Ashurbanipal (668–627 B.C.E.), king of Assyria, feasting in a leafy garden with his queen, attended by servants and musicians. The unique feature of this scene is the position of the king, who is reclining on a bed; ordinarily participants in a feast would be sitting upright. Until this time, whenever a king celebrated a victory he was represented in a seated position. The king is holding a lotus flower in his left hand as he drinks from a bowl; the queen too is drinking from a bowl. A panel depicting the "woman at the window" ornaments the bed. Richard Barnett, who made a lifelong study of the ivories of the ancient Near East, interpreted this banquet scene as both a *marzeah* and a victory celebration. The ivory bed decorated with panels of the "woman at the window" would conform to the *marzeah* ritual in Syria and Phoenicia.

In the estimation of Amos the ivory beds used in the *marzeah*, together with all the other ivories, symbolized everything that was wrong with Israelite society. They stood for lush prosperity, social injustice, callous selfishness, and pagan immorality. While many were living in poverty, the wealthy class was enjoying great affluence, often achieved by oppression of the impoverished. Also, ivory panels adorned with

Ashurbanipal feasting in a garden. Found in the palace at Nineveh, this relief represents the king of Assyria reclining in a garden while feasting with his queen. They are drinking to the sound of music. The reclining position of the king is a unique depiction in Neo-Assyrian art. (*Courtesy of the Trustees of the British Museum*)

images would have been a serious transgression of the Second Commandment, which forbids graven images.

Apart from religious and moral considerations, the ivories imported from Phoenicia bearing Egyptianizing motifs attest to the cosmopolitan culture of eighth-century Israel. No longer were the people of Samaria living in isolation; they had become more open to the culture of their neighbors, even though much of what it represented ran counter to their own religious tradition.

Calves from the Midst of the Stall

The phrase "calves from the midst of the stall" refers to stall-fattened, tender calves. The Hebrew word *marbeq* ("stall") designates an enclosure where animals were restrained for fattening. On the basis of recent excavations, some archaeologists are convinced that the domestic stables were located within, not separate from, the houses. These houses were pillared buildings, usually divided into three sections, with troughs constructed between the pillars. In the eighth century B.C.E., stables of this kind could be found at sites such as Megiddo, Beer-sheba, Hazor, and Tell es-Saidiyeh (in Jordan).

Perhaps the best-known buildings at Megiddo are the stables with their hitching posts. Philip Guy, second director of the University of Chicago excavations at Megiddo, identified these buildings as the stables of Solomon. In the 1960s, Yigael Yadin, distinguished Israeli archaeologist, established that the stable compound at Megiddo dated later than the Solomonic period (961–922 B.C.E.) and perhaps was contemporary with King Ahab's reign (869–850 B.C.E.).

As Yadin had reconsidered the date of the Megiddo stables, James Pritchard reassessed the function of these pillared buildings. Rejecting the "stable interpretation," he suggested they were storehouses or barracks. He objected that the huge mangerlike ashlar blocks within the pillared buildings at Megiddo were too shallow (six inches deep) to hold grain or fodder for horses. Pritchard argued also that horses were not kept in stables but in open enclosures. Further, he objected that the rough stones in the area of the stalls, instead of preventing the horses' hooves from slipping, would have had an adverse effect on the hooves. In addition, Pritchard interpreted the holes in the corners of the Megiddo pillars as devices for securing drag ropes when the pillars were being transported.

In a recent study of horses and stables in the ancient Near East, John Holladay[2] presents evidence from archaeology, epigraphy (inscriptions), and iconography (pictorial material) concerning the care of horses in antiquity. He concludes that the architectural features of the tripartite buildings at Megiddo, Beer-sheba, Hazor, and elsewhere, in the light of the physical requirements of stabled horses, indicate that these buildings were constructed specifically for the housing and conditioning of war-horses. Troughs or mangers fixed in the low walls between the columns have been uncovered at several sites. These broad, shallow mangers, reaching the height of the animal's chest, would have been ideal for feeding, according to Holladay's research. He concludes that in the ancient Near East horses were kept in stables, not in open enclosures.

Building on Holladay's analysis of public stables, Lawrence Stager[3] draws convincing conclusions with respect to domestic stables. In Iron Age I and II (1200–586 B.C.E.), pillared houses with two, three, or four rooms were the common style of domestic dwellings. Artifacts recovered from these buildings indicate that they were the domiciles of farmers and herders. Architectural features at et-Tell, identified as the biblical city of Ai, about eight miles north of Jerusalem, suggest that animals were sheltered within the houses, with the ground floor of the covered siderooms serving as stables. These siderooms were usually paved with flagstone; hard pavement is desirable for toughening the hooves of animals, which was especially important for horses before the invention of the horseshoe, as Stager points out. Just as the large, pillared buildings constructed on a tripartite plan in Iron Age II were suitable for stabling horses, so too the more modest domestic buildings of Iron Age I had the same capability with respect to ventilation, stalls, mangers, tethering devices, and other considerations.

Mangers in Iron Age II domestic stables have been excavated at Tell es-Saidiyeh, Lachish, and Hazor. At Tell es-Saidiyeh, probably biblical Zarethan in the Jordan Valley, Pritchard excavated mangers built into the stylobates (continuous bases supporting rows of columns) of pillared walls of houses. According to his description, "In the spans between the four mudbrick columns and the two pilasters (rectangular columns) that supported the roof of House 6 are basins constructed of rows of rubble stone and plastered with mud."[4]

The best illustration of stables located within a building is from Kurnub, perhaps the Roman and Byzantine city of Mampsis, a Negev site twenty-five miles southeast of Beer-sheba. One of the Nabatean public buildings, dating to the first half of the second century c.e., had three rooms arranged in basilical form, namely, a wide nave set between two elongated rooms. The western and eastern walls of the central hall had doors and four arched windows. Mangers built into the sills of these windows suggest that the elongated rooms functioned as stables.

The foregoing archaeological evidence is useful for understanding several biblical references to the "calves from the midst of the stall" or fatted calves. The witch of Endor served Saul a meal consisting of a stall-fed calf which she had in the house (1 Sam. 28:24). The prodigal son in Luke's Gospel was served the same menu upon his return home (Luke 15:23–27).

Eating "calves from the midst of the stall" was for Amos another indication of high living by the self-indulgent people of Samaria. This epicurean dish, together with "lambs from the flock," was listed among the principal components of the *marzeah*.

The Sound of the Harp

Music played a vital role in the life of ancient people, so it is not surprising that the Bible contains many references to musical instruments. Also, excavations at Hazor, Beth-shan, Megiddo, Ashdod, and Jerusalem have contributed valuable evidence about musical instruments in antiquity.

According to the *Encyclopaedia Judaica:* "The Bible is the foremost and richest source for knowledge of the musical life of ancient Israel until some time after the return from the Babylonian Exile. It is complemented by several external sources: archaeological relics of musical instruments and of depictions of musical scenes; comparative material from the neighboring cultures; and post-biblical sources."[5]

Stable at Kurnub. Illustrated are the Late Nabatean (first half of the second century C.E.) stable, *top,* and troughs, *next page,* at Kurnub (Mampsis). The public building consisted of three rooms arranged in the form of a basilica: a wide nave between two aisles. In the walls of the central hall were four arched windows with mangers built into the sills of the arched windows, indicating that the side aisles served as stables. *(Courtesy of the Expedition to Kurnub, Abraham Negev, Director; drawings by Douglas Gilbert)*

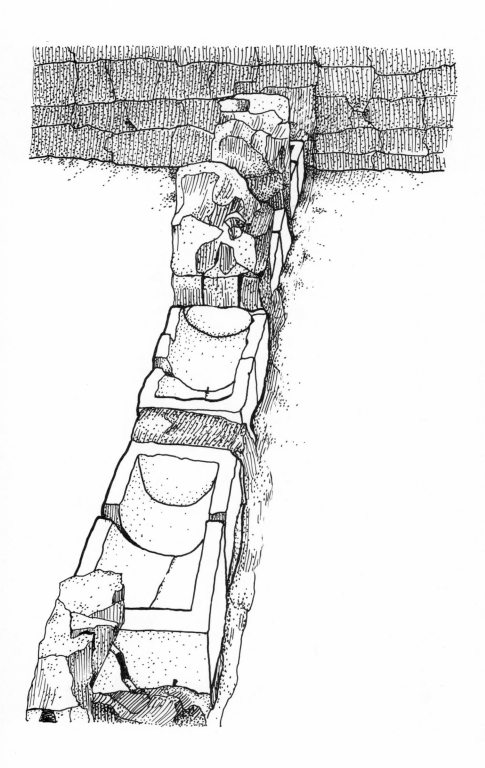

The neighboring cultures have provided comparative material of extreme value for understanding the musical heritage of the ancient Near East. Babylonia and Assyria have made the most important contributions, especially the reliefs commemorating the triumphs of their victorious kings. Typical are the relief sculptures of musicians and singers from the seventy-room royal palace of Sennacherib (704–681 B.C.E.) at Kuyunjik, one of the two great mounds marking the 1,800-acre site of ancient Nineveh, opposite modern Mosul in Iraq. The bas-reliefs in Sennacherib's palace (later occupied by Esarhaddon [680–669 B.C.E.] and Ashurbanipal [668–627 B.C.E.]) covered almost two miles of halls and galleries.

Despite such rich resources and the growing knowledge of ancient music during the past three decades, much remains uncertain. Through the centuries Hebrew musical terms have been translated erroneously; even modern versions of the Bible render these terms variously. Rabbinic writers sometimes had difficulty in determining whether a musical term referred to a stringed or a wind instrument.

Stringed instruments figure prominently in the Bible. The *kinnor* and the *nebel* are the only stringed instruments mentioned in the Old Testament; frequently they are named together. Commentators count forty-two references to the *kinnor* in the Bible, and twenty-seven to the *nebel*. About the nature of these instruments scholarly opinion diverges greatly, but some general observations can be made.

Stringed instruments were made of wood, although some would say silver or ivory. The *kinnor* and the *nebel* are two different types of lyres, the *nebel* being the larger of the two and perhaps the more solemn instrument for liturgical use. The fact that *nebel* may also signify "leather bottle" or "jar" may account for the bulky shape of the musical instrument. The *kinnor*, consisting of a body, two arms, and a yoke, is asymmetrical, with one arm shorter than the other. *Kinnor* should be translated "lyre," not "harp"; it did not belong to the family of harps. Utilized for both sacred and secular purposes, the *kinnor* was the instrument of David and the Levites. The number of strings on the *kinnor* varies between three and twelve; the *nebel* has twelve strings.

In describing the musical component of the *marzeah*, Amos uses the word *nebel* (Amos 6:5) for the instrument, ordinarily reserved for a religious function. The verb accompanying the noun is *parat* (literally, "to pluck fruit"), suggesting that the *nebel* was plucked with the fingers.

Amos, citing the Lord, uses *nebel* in one other place: "Take away from me the noise of your songs; to the melody of your harps (*nebel*) I will not listen" (Amos 5:23). This divine condemnation is uttered as part of God's total rejection of Israel's worship. The occasion was a combination of feast and a sacrifice, consisting of eating meat, of singing, and of playing the *nebel*, a setting not unlike the *marzeaḥ* described in Amos 6:4–5.

Because of ambiguity in the translation of the Hebrew text, confusion has arisen between the lyre and the harp. The Revised Standard Version (used in this book) is probably not accurate in rendering *nebel* as "harp." To date, no example of the harp has been uncovered from Syria-Palestine. A basic distinction between the two instruments is the yoke or crossbar: the lyre has a yoke, the harp does not. According to Anne Kilmer, authority on the music of the ancient Near East, the lyre has two arms, often of unequal length, rising from the sound box. The strings are attached to the yoke at the top of the instrument. The harp has but one arm rising from the sound box. The strings of the harp are of differing lengths; the strings of the lyre are of the same length.

Among the pictorial representations of lyres in the ancient Near East, besides the victory scene on the ivory panel from Megiddo, another should be mentioned. At Kuntillet Ajrud, a wayside shrine of the early eighth century B.C.E. in the Sinai, a drawing on one of the *pithoi* (storage jars) depicts a lyre player, a figure seated on a chair and holding a musical instrument, identified as an asymmetrical *kinnor*. Pirhiya Beck, who has made a detailed study of the drawings from Kuntillet Ajrud, points out that the motif of a single lyre player is well known from eighth-century seals. (See page 105.)

Seals have an important contribution to make to the understanding of culture and history. The large number of seals from the eighth through the sixth century B.C.E. points to an increase of literacy in that period. Both private and official seals were applied to small lumps of clay which in turn were affixed to documents as a way of securing them. In case of fire the papyrus would have been consumed, but the seal impression on the clay bulla would have withstood the flames.

One of the most beautifully crafted seals, dating to the seventh century B.C.E. but of unknown origin, bears the tantalizing Hebrew inscription: "(Belonging) to Maadanah, the king's daughter." This is the first occurrence of the name Maadanah, derived from a Hebrew root meaning "delight," in the history of Israel; she is not further identified, nor is her father, the king. This seal indicates that at least some women acted in their own name with respect to legal matters in ancient Israel. What makes this tiny scaraboid seal of brown jasper especially memorable is the delicate design of a *kinnor* which decorates it. The lyre is asymmetrical, consisting of a sound box and two unequal arms with twelve strings attached to a yoke. A string of pearls adorns the outer edge of the sound box, with a rosette in the center. The king's daughter most likely chose the lyre as her emblem because she played this instrument.

A poignant representation of three lyre players appears on an Assyrian relief from Nineveh commemorating Sennacherib's conquest of Lachish in 701 B.C.E. These Judahite prisoners of war are depicted playing their lyres as they move through the mountains guarded by an Assyrian soldier armed with a club and a bow.

Two wind instruments, the shofar and the trumpet (*ḥaṣoṣerah*), are mentioned by Amos and Hosea. The shofar may be identical with the keren (its original meaning being the "horn" of an animal). The shofar, adopted from the Assyrians and in common use in Israel from earliest times, was made from the horn of either a ram or a wild goat. Still used in Jewish liturgy, the shofar is the most frequently mentioned

Seal of Maadanah. This brown jasper seal, scaraboid in shape and beautifully executed, dates to the seventh century B.C.E. The lyre on the seal closely resembles David's instrument. *(N. Avigad, "The King's Daughter and the Lyre," Israel Exploration Journal 28 [1978]:146–151; courtesy of Nahman Avigad; drawing by Douglas Gilbert)*

musical instrument in the Bible, beginning with Ex. 19:16, where the shofar signals the great theophany at Sinai. Some would say that it is not a musical instrument, because its purpose is to make noise, not music. It was also used for signaling in war and in peace. Amos mentions blasts from the shofar in his description of the destruction of Moab (Amos 2:2). In Hos. 8:1 a military officer is commanded to sound the alarm with the shofar to warn of imminent danger. Precise instructions were laid down for blowing the shofar. On an Iron Age II basalt relief from Carchemish, a center of Hittite culture on the Euphrates River (just inside the Turkish border from Syria), musicians are depicted playing a curved horn or shofar and a drum.

The trumpet is well known from its representation on the Arch of

Three captive musicians. An alabaster relief adorning the palace of Sennacherib at Nineveh depicts three barefoot captives plucking the strings of their lyres with a plectrum on the way to captivity in Assyria under the watchful eye of their Assyrian guard. These musicians bear a striking resemblance to the figures depicted in the siege of Lachish; therefore they may be Judahites. *(Courtesy of the Trustees of the British Museum; drawing by Douglas Gilbert)*

Triumph erected in Rome by the emperor Titus after the destruction of the Temple of Jerusalem in 70 c.e. Based on Egyptian models, the trumpet, made of beaten silver or other metal, is a long, straight instrument without valves. Used in pairs, trumpets were the musical instrument par excellence of the priests. Toward the end of the eighth century b.c.e. both the horn and the trumpet were used for signaling. Numbers 10:2–10 gives details about the manner of sounding the trumpet on various occasions.

To warn of imminent attack during the Syro-Israelite war of 735–734 b.c.e., Hosea sounds a frantic alarm: "Blow the horn *(shofar)* in Gibeah, the trumpet *(ḥaṣoṣerah)* in Ramah" (Hos. 5:8). The Judahite reprisal against Israel, specifically against the towns of Gibeah and Ramah in the Northern Kingdom, is being described in this verse.

Wine in Bowls

Inordinate consumption of wine is enumerated as the fourth element of the *marzeaḥ*. In such a context the Hebrew word *mizraq*, used here to designate a wine bowl, is unusual. Its root is *zrq,* meaning "to throw," "to sprinkle" (dust, ashes, water, blood). In the ceremony of covenant ratification at Sinai, according to the ritual: "Moses took half of the blood and put it in basins, and half of the blood he threw *(zrq)* against the altar" (Ex. 24:6). A *mizraq* is a dish or basin used for sprinkling, so it must have had a wide mouth. It is mentioned frequently in the Old Testament in the context of cult, as in this example from the Book of Exodus.

In the description of the altar of burnt offering and its accessories, it is required: "You shall make pots for it [the altar of burnt offering] to receive its ashes, and shovels and basins *(mizraq)* and forks and firepans; all its utensils you shall make of bronze" (Ex. 27:3). Concerning the offerings from the tribal leaders for the service of the tabernacle and the dedication of the altar, it is related: "His [Nahshon's] offering was one silver plate whose weight was a hundred and thirty shekels, one silver basin *(mizraq)* of seventy shekels, according to the shekel of the sanctuary, both of them full of fine flour mixed with oil for a cereal offering" (Num. 7:13).

It is not certain whether the *mizraq* in Amos' description was ceramic or metal ware. If he had in mind the ritual "basin" described in the books of Exodus and Numbers, the ware was metal. If it was ceramic ware, Amos may have been referring to the large four-handled ring-burnished banquet bowl of Iron Age II. However, in libation scenes depicted in ancient art the vessels are usually bowls without handles.

Some bowls in the category of *mizraq* are quite capacious, with a diameter of eighteen inches. Amos may have mentioned the use of sacred vessels at the *marzeah* to underscore its sacrilegious nature. Also, he may have mentioned the use of vessels of large capacity to emphasize that inordinate drinking was an integral part of the *marzeah.*

The discovery of a fluted bronze bowl *(phiale)* with a Phoenician dedicatory inscription may cast some light on the kind of drinking container used in the *marzeah.* The bowl in question is of uncertain origin but is said to have originated in modern Lebanon. Dating from the fourth century B.C.E., it measures seven inches in diameter and is quite shallow, only an inch and a half high. It is described as having a sixteen-petaled rosette at bottom center. This bowl lacks handles, just as other bowls depicted in libation scenes, namely, Ashurbanipal feasting in the garden while reclining and the Canaanite prince seated on a throne at a victory feast, drinking from a bowl.

This class of fluted bowl was in use during the Persian period (538–332 B.C.E.) and has Assyrian prototypes that date to Amos' time, when Israel was under Assyrian rule. The truly important feature of this bronze *phiale* is the inscription: "we offer two cups to the marzeah of

Shamash." The reference to "marzeah" and the specific mention of the "marzeah of Shamash," the sun-god of the Semitic pantheon, give a few more clues about the nature of the *marzeaḥ.* [6]

The Finest Oils

Now that archaeologists are aware of the importance of collecting paleobotanical specimens, much more is known today about agriculture in the ancient Near East. Mentioned more than two hundred times in the Bible, olive oil is both a necessity of life and, as Hosea points out, a gift of God (Hos. 2:8). Second in importance to the production of wine, oil was a major industry of ancient Israel and a significant export. In contrast, olives were not grown in Egypt and Mesopotamia. Alluding to the prosperity of the oil merchants, Hosea says, "They make a bargain with Assyria, and oil is carried to Egypt" (Hos. 12:1). The many stone olive presses found recently through survey and excavation in modern Israel—for example, at Tel Miqne (Ekron), Tel Batash (Timnah), and Tel Dan (Dan)—are adding considerably to the large number of presses already known.

Touching on so many aspects of life, olive oil had multiple uses in biblical times: in food preparation, as an unguent for softening the skin, in offering sacrifice, as fuel for lamps, for medicinal purposes, for the preparation of cosmetics, and as a lubricant. The olive tree, still plentiful in the Mediterranean region, can survive for a thousand years and continue to produce fruit, harvested in September and October.

The prime foe of the olive tree is the locust. In a litany of disasters that plagued Israel, Amos includes the locusts: "Your fig trees and your olive trees the locust devoured" (Amos 4:9). Among the sanctions for Jerusalem's breaking the covenant, Micah includes what Delbert Hillers calls "futility curses"[7]: "You shall sow, but not reap; you shall tread olives, but not anoint yourselves with oil; you shall tread grapes, but not drink wine" (Micah 6:15).

The stages in the extraction of olive oil are crushing and pressing; they are two separate operations. Crushing, which consists in grinding the olives into a soft paste, is achieved by rolling a large stone (the crushing stone, or *memel*) over the olives spread on a flat surface of rock or on the floor of a shallow basin *(yam)*. Another method of crushing the olive is mentioned in the Micah text, just cited: treading or trampling the olive. Then the pulp is pressed to extract the oil by putting the crushed olives into woven baskets (*'aqalim*) with holes in the bottom. The baskets, covered with a stone, are placed on the pressing surface. Pressure is exerted on the olives by a long beam weighted with stones and secured in a wall niche located behind the presses and the

Olive press installation at Tel Miqne. This is one of over a hundred such installations dating to the seventh century B.C.E. that have been uncovered at Tel Miqne (Ekron). Shown in the reconstruction of the olive press are the crushing basin (1), the presses (2), the stone weights (3), and the wooden lever (4). *(Courtesy of the Joint Excavation Project, Trude Dothan and Seymour Gitin, Directors; photo by Douglas Guthrie; reconstruction by Erez Cohen)*

crushing basin. The olive oil flows through the basket openings into a groove, then through a channel in the rock into the central vat or bowl. This type of oil press installation was used extensively in Iron Age II.

Tel Miqne, identified with the Philistine city of Ekron, is one of the largest Iron Age sites to be excavated in modern Israel. In Iron Age II, specifically the seventh century B.C.E., Ekron was one of the most important olive oil production centers in the entire Near East. As mentioned already, more than one hundred olive oil press installations have been found there. Apparently the Philistines at Ekron processed their own oil so as to be self-sufficient. Most of the presses uncovered at Tel Miqne were equipped with a larger than customary pressing surface and central collecting vat, yielding more than twice as many liters of oil as the simpler presses. A satisfactory explanation has not yet been given.

The first crushing, done in a vat before the pressing process, yields oil of the finest quality. The prepressed oil is the best oil, also called the virgin oil. Stager[8] explains the production of "the finest oils" used in the *marzeaḥ* in this way. He notes that the Samaria ostraca mention many times *shemen raḥuṣ* (literally, "washed oil"). This refers to a technique for extracting olive oil. Water was poured over the crushed olives, the mixture was stirred, and the floating oil was skimmed off by hand. Olives that are not completely crushed when the water is poured over them can be further squeezed by hand while in the water-filled basin. The result was the virgin oil or "the finest oils."

Bedrock cavities, channels, and basins excavated in the Samaria region may have been utilized in the process of crushing and pressing olives and may have been the source of "the finest oils" with which the wealthy of Samaria anointed themselves as part of the *marzeaḥ* ritual.

Notes

Preface

1. H. D. Lance, *The Old Testament and the Archaeologist* (Philadelphia: Fortress Press, 1981), p. 48.

2. P. King, "Amos," "Micah," in *The Jerome Biblical Commentary*, ed. R. E. Brown, J. Fitzmyer, and R. Murphy (Englewood Cliffs, N.J.: Prentice-Hall, 1968), pp. 242–252, 283–289.

Introduction

1. W. Albright, "The Impact of Archaeology on Biblical Research—1966," in *New Directions in Biblical Archaeology*, ed. D. N. Freedman and J. Greenfield (Garden City, N.Y.: Doubleday & Co., 1971), pp. 3–4.

2. C. Renfrew, *Approaches to Social Archaeology* (Cambridge: Harvard University Press, 1984).

Chapter 1: Archaeology and the Eighth-Century Prophets

1. Y. Yadin, *Hazor II: An Account of the Second Season of Excavations*, 1956, 1960 (Jerusalem: Magnes Press, 1960), p. 24.

2. Balaam, probably an Ammonite, was summoned by Balak, king of Moab, to curse the Israelites (Num. 22:6), but he could only bless Israel. In 1967 archaeologists discovered at Tell Deir Alla in the middle Jordan Valley, east of the Jordan River, fragments of wall plaster inscribed in a Northwest Semitic dialect referring to "Balaam, son of Beor, seer of the gods." Undoubtedly this is the same Balaam described in Numbers 22 to 24. This plaster, mural inscription from Deir Alla dates to the mid-eighth century B.C.E. The stratum in which the plaster fragments were found was destroyed by a severe earthquake, which some identify with the earthquake mentioned in Amos 1:1.

Chapter 3: Architecture, Fortifications, and Warfare

1. Y. Shiloh, *The Proto-Aeolic Capital and Israelite Ashlar Masonry* (Jerusalem: Institute of Archaeology, Hebrew University, 1979), p. 61.

2. M. Dayagi-Mendels, in *Treasures of the Holy Land: Ancient Art from the Israel Museum* (New York: Metropolitan Museum of Art, 1986), p. 170.

3. S. Lloyd, *The Archaeology of Mesopotamia: From the Old Stone Age to the Persian Conquest* (London: Thames & Hudson, 1978); J. Reade, *Assyrian Sculpture* (London: British Museum Publications, 1983), pp. 5–12.

4. D. Ussishkin, *The Conquest of Lachish by Sennacherib* (Tel Aviv: Institute of Archaeology, Tel Aviv University, 1982), p. 11.

5. I. Ephal, "The Assyrian Siege Ramp at Lachish: Military and Linguistic Aspects," *Tel Aviv* 11 (1984): 60–70.

6. Ibid.

Chapter 4: Cult in Israel and Judah

1. R. de Vaux, *Ancient Israel: Its Life and Institutions* (New York: McGraw-Hill Book Co., 1961), p. 272.

2. C. Graesser, "Standing Stones in Ancient Palestine," *The Biblical Archaeologist* 35 (1972): 34–63.

3. M. Coogan, "Of Cult and Cultures: Reflections on the Interpretation of Archaeological Evidence," *Palestine Exploration Quarterly* 119 (1987): 1–8.

4. M. Coogan, "Canaanite Origins and Lineage: Reflections on the Religion of Ancient Israel," in *Ancient Israelite Religion: Essays in Honor of Frank Moore Cross,* ed. P. Miller, Jr., P. Hanson, and S. D. McBride (Philadelphia: Fortress Press, 1987), p. 119.

5. D. N. Freedman, "Yahweh of Samaria and His Asherah," presentation at International Meeting of the Society of Biblical Literature, Heidelberg (W. Germany), August 11, 1987 (to be published).

6. R. Hestrin, "The Cult Stand from Taanach and Its Religious Background," *Studia Phoenicia* V, ed. E. Lipinski (Louvain: Uitgeverij Peeters, 1987), pp. 61–77.

Chapter 5: Agriculture, Plants, and Animals

1. M. Zohary, *Plants of the Bible* (Cambridge: Cambridge University Press, 1982), p. 36.

2. N. Hareuveni, *Tree and Shrub in Our Biblical Heritage* (Kiryat Ono: Neot Kedumim, 1984), pp. 90–92.

3. J. Ross, "Wine," *The Interpreter's Dictionary of the Bible* (New York: Abingdon Press, 1962), 4: 849–852.

4. Zohary, *Plants of the Bible,* p. 104.

5. Hareuveni, *Tree and Shrub,* p. 73.

6. P. Miller, "Animal Names as Designations in Ugaritic and Hebrew," *Ugarit-Forschungen* 2 (1970): 177–186.

7. D. Hill, "The Animal Fountain of Araq el-Emir," *Bulletin of the American Schools of Oriental Research* 171 (1963): 45–55.

8. G. R. Driver, "Birds in the Old Testament: Birds in Life," *Palestine Exploration Quarterly* 87 (1955): 129.

9. N. Avigad, "A Hebrew Seal with a Family Emblem," *Israel Exploration Journal* 16 (1966): 52.

Chapter 6: The *Marzeaḥ*: Banquets and High Living

1. I. Winter, "Ivory Carving," in *Ebla to Damascus: Art and Archaeology of Ancient Syria,* ed. H. Weiss (Washington, D.C.: Smithsonian Institution, 1985), pp. 343–344.

2. J. Holladay, "The Stables of Ancient Israel," in *The Archaeology of Jordan and Other Studies,* ed. L. Geraty and L. Herr (Berrien Springs, Mich.: Andrews University Press, 1986), pp. 103–165.

3. L. Stager, "The Archaeology of the Family in Ancient Israel," *Bulletin of the American Schools of Oriental Research* 260 (1985): 1–35.

4. J. Pritchard, "The Megiddo Stables: A Reassessment," in *Near Eastern Archaeology in the Twentieth Century: Essays in Honor of Nelson Glueck,* ed. J. Sanders (Garden City, N.Y.: Doubleday & Co., 1970), p. 272.

5. B. Bayer, "Music," *Encyclopaedia Judaica* (New York: Macmillan Co., 1972), Vol. 12, p. 559.

6. N. Avigad and J. Greenfield, "A Bronze *phialē* with a Phoenician Dedicatory Inscription," *Israel Exploration Journal* 32 (1982): 118–128.

7. D. Hillers, *Micah,* Hermeneia (Philadelphia: Fortress Press, 1984), p. 82.

8. L. Stager, "The Finest Olive Oil in Samaria," *Journal of Semitic Studies* 28 (1983): 241–245.

Glossary

acropolis: A defensible hilltop constituting the fortified center of a city.

adytum: The innermost sanctuary in an ancient temple.

ashlar masonry: Rectangular blocks of cut stone.

balustrade: A series of pillars or columns supporting a handrail.

broadhouse: A building whose focal point is situated on the long wall.

bulla: A seal impression on clay or other material.

capital: The uppermost member of a column or pillar.

casemate wall: A double wall with a narrow space between, divided by partitions with small chambers used for storage or filled with earth to strengthen the wall.

Chalcolithic period: The copper-stone age (4200–3300 B.C.E.), when copper and stone tools and weapons were used simultaneously.

epigraphy: The study of ancient written remains, dating and interpreting them.

faience: Earthenware decorated with opaque colored glazes.

fosse: A dry moat or ditch.

glacis: A sloping bank or rampart built of dirt, stone, and other materials.

header-stretcher: Header is a stone laid perpendicular to the face of a wall; stretcher is a stone laid with its side parallel to the face of the wall.

hekal: In Hebrew it designates the palace of a god.

khirbet: In Arabic it designates an ancient site with ruins.

maṣṣebah: An upright stone, usually associated with sacred rites.

offset-inset wall: A type of city wall constructed in such a way that one section protrudes and the next is recessed.

ostracon: A piece of pottery with writing on it.

pentapolis: A confederation or group of five cities.

potsherd: A fragment of pottery.

rosette: A carved or molded conventional rose used for decoration.

Shephelah: A low-lying plain located between the East Mediterranean coast and the Judean hills in modern Israel.

stele (stela): An upright slab or stone column with a decoration or inscription.

stratigraphy: Analysis of the sequence of layers on a tell.

syncretism: Mixture of conflicting beliefs or practices.

tell, tel: An artificial mound built up from the remains of successive settlements.

temenos: A sacred precinct.

wadi: In Arabic the bed of a valley or stream that is dry except in the rainy season.

Selected Bibliography

Chapter 1: Archaeology and the Eighth-Century Prophets

Archaeology

Aharoni, Yohanan. *The Archaeology of the Land of Israel.* Translated by Anson F. Rainey. Philadelphia: Westminster Press, 1978.

King, Philip J. *American Archaeology in the Mideast: A History of the American Schools of Oriental Research.* Philadelphia: American Schools of Oriental Research, 1983.

Lance, H. Darrell. *The Old Testament and the Archaeologist.* Philadelphia: Fortress Press, 1981.

Mazar, Benjamin, and Hershel Shanks, eds. *Recent Archaeology in the Land of Israel.* Washington, D.C.: Biblical Archaeology Society, 1984.

Prophetism

Blenkinsopp, Joseph. *A History of Prophecy in Israel.* Philadelphia: Westminster Press, 1983.

Mays, James L. *Amos, A Commentary.* Philadelphia: Westminster Press, 1969.

———. *Hosea, A Commentary.* Philadelphia: Westminster Press, 1969.

———. *Micah, A Commentary.* Philadelphia: Westminster Press, 1976.

Chapter 2: Historical and Geographical Setting

History

Bright, John. *A History of Israel.* 3d ed. Philadelphia: Westminster Press, 1981.

Miller, J. Maxwell, and John H. Hayes. *A History of Ancient Israel and Judah.* Philadelphia: Westminster Press, 1986.

Geography

Aharoni, Yohanan. *The Land of the Bible: A Historical Geography.* Rev. and enlarged ed. Philadelphia: Westminster Press, 1979.

Baly, Denis. *The Geography of the Bible.* 2d ed. New York: Harper & Row, 1979.

Chapter 3: Architecture, Fortifications, and Warfare

Architecture

Shiloh, Yigal. *The Proto-Aeolic Capital and Israelite Ashlar Masonry.* Jerusalem: Institute of Archaeology, Hebrew University, 1979.

Fortifications and Warfare

Ussishkin, David. *The Conquest of Lachish by Sennacherib.* Tel Aviv: Institute of Archaeology, Tel Aviv University, 1982.
de Vaux, Roland. *Ancient Israel: Its Life and Institutions.* New York: McGraw-Hill Book Co., 1961. Pp. 213–267.
Yadin, Yigael. *The Art of Warfare in Biblical Lands.* New York: McGraw-Hill Book Co., 1963.

Chapter 4: Cult in Israel and Judah

Miller, Patrick D., Jr., Paul D. Hanson, and S. Dean McBride, eds. *Ancient Israelite Religion: Essays in Honor of Frank Moore Cross.* Philadelphia: Fortress Press, 1987.
de Vaux, Roland. *Ancient Israel: Its Life and Institutions.* New York: McGraw-Hill Book Co., 1961. Pp. 271–517.

Chapter 5: Agriculture, Plants, and Animals

Agriculture

Borowski, Oded. *Agriculture in Iron Age Israel: The Evidence from Archaeology and the Bible.* Winona Lake, Ind.: Eisenbrauns, 1987.

Plants

Hareuveni, Nogah. *Tree and Shrub in Our Biblical Heritage.* Kiryat Ono: Neot Kedumim, 1984.
Zohary, Michael. *Plants of the Bible.* Cambridge: Cambridge University Press, 1982.

Animals

Bodenheimer, Friedrich S. *Animal and Man in Bible Lands.* Leiden: E. J. Brill, 1960.
Cansdale, George S. *All the Animals of the Bible Lands.* Grand Rapids: Zondervan, 1970.

Chapter 6: The *Marzeaḥ:* Banquets and High Living

Marzeaḥ

Greenfield, Jonas. "The *Marzeaḥ* as a Social Institution." *Acta Antiqua* (Budapest) 22 (1974), pp. 451–455.

Pope, Marvin H. "A Divine Banquet at Ugarit." In *The Use of the Old Testament in the New,* edited by J. Efird, pp. 170–203. Durham: Duke University, 1972.
———. "The Cult of the Dead at Ugarit." In *Ugarit in Retrospect: Fifty Years of Ugarit and Ugaritic,* edited by Gordon Young, pp. 159–179. Winona Lake, Ind.: Eisenbrauns, 1981.

Ivory

Barnett, Richard D. *Ancient Ivories in the Middle East.* Jerusalem: Institute of Archaeology, 1982.

Music

Sendrey, Alfred. *Music in Ancient Israel.* New York: Philosophical Library, 1969.

Selected Index

Scripture Index